The
Irving Berlin
Songography
1907–1966

The
IRVING BERLIN
SONGOGRAPHY
1907–1966

by

DAVE JAY

Arlington House   *New Rochelle, N.Y.*

PREFACE

by Dave Jay

Let's delve into some of the least explored facets
of the Berlin genius. I'm intrigued by his talent
for writing lyrics that are simultaneously timely
and timeless. Sing the verse of "Smile and Show
Your Dimple", it's a song cheering up a girl whose
fellow has marched away to World War I; sing only
the chorus, it's a cheer-up song good any year.
The verse of "I'll See You in C-U-B-A" renders
it an anti-prohibition ditty typical of 1920;
drop the verse and it becomes just a travelogue
number not rendered obsolete until the fiendish
emergence of Castro. During World War II, when
a common enemy forced us into a temporary alliance
with Soviet Russia, that country was propagandized
favorably by many who were unfairly called upon
to answer for it during the McCarthy era. Berlin
was more far-sighted. His song, "That Russian
Winter", praised the Commies' weather - never
their people.

Berlin's greatest gift, though, is his ability
to write for great artists in such a way as not
only to showcase their individual style and song-
projection, but to enhance it. How outstandingly
this genius was displayed in the drollery of
"Woodman, Woodman, Spare That Tree" (for Bert
Williams), the exhuberant suggestiveness of
"You'd Be Surprised" (for Eddie Cantor), the
staccato rhythm of "Puttin' On The Ritz" (for
Harry Richman), the insouciance of "I'll Capture
Your Heart" and "A Couple of Song and Dance Men"

(for Bing Crosby and Fred Astaire). Though Berlin
hadn't written these songs for these artists, it
was equally apropos that he suggested Donald
O'Connor revive "What Chance Have I With Love"
(in "Call Me Madam", 1953), Tony Martin revive
"Maybe I Love You Too Much" (on TV, September
12, 1951) and Al Jolson revive "The Call Of The
South" (in "Mammy", 1930).

It was in his songs for this latter film – the
greatest writer of songs composing for the very
greatest singer of songs – that Berlin reached
his zenith. "Let Me Sing And I'm Happy" not only
is Jolson set to music – the philosophy and its
realization that made him The World's Greatest
Entertainer – but is one of the best songs ever
written, the most perfect example of that pure
Berlin genius that perfectly blends lyrics and
melodies (again, not only showcasing but enhanc-
ing each other) to carry and develop a single
idea, simple, directly, dramatically, from start
to finish. Berlin has never written a song in
which he didn't do this. His least successful
numbers are intrinsically superior to the biggest
hits of nearly anyone else.

FOREWORD

by Dave Jay

Known recordings of each song, listed beneath its
title, omit recordings of that song included in
album collections of Irving Berlin songs, since
all of these are itemized as conclusion of the
Songography. Albums of selections from each
Berlin show or film, "original cast" and "sound-
track" or otherwise, are itemized directly following that show or film. Each recording (of those
listed individually) is followed by its rpm
speed (78, 45, 33-1/3) in parenthesis; and if
it sold a million or more copies, by an asterick
(*). Layout of entire Berlin Songography was
made easier by having compiled "JOLSONOGRAPHY".

Marie From Sunny Italy
  (melody by Nick Nicholson)
  Other than earlier unpublished parodies on then-
  current George M. Cohan and Harry Von Tilzer
  hits, written that he might perform them for
  the patrons of Nigger Mike Salter's saloon, this
  was singing waiter Izzy Baline's first song.
  Salter ordered it written to compete with
  Callahan's whose pianist, Al Piantadosi, had
  just written the hit "My Muriuccia Take a Steam-
  boat" (lyrics by George Ranklyn). When the
  sheet music erroneously printed his name as
  "I. Berlin", he retained the last; deciding that
  "Israel" sounded too pompous, "Izzy" too ornery,
  he changed the first to Irving. The verse contained such rhymes as "queen" with "mandolin",
  "patiently" with "happy be", "beauty" with "suit
  me", for which Berlin's share of the 75 cents
  royalties came to 37 cents. But it was the first
  step in a journey to immortality.
      Joe Brenner (Fred Hall), Coronet CX-97
                    (33-1/3)

                    1908:

The Best of Friends Must Part
  Berlin's second song, and the first for which he
  wrote both lyrics and melody.
Queenie (My Own)
  (melody was by Maurice Abrahams)
She Was A Dear Little Girl
  Interpolated in Marie Cahill show "The Boys And
  Betty".

7

Dorando
  A topical song in Italian dialect, dealing with
  Dorando's defeat by Johnny Longboat in the 1908
  Olympic Marathon.
Just Like The Rose
  (melody by Al Piantadosi)
Oh! What I Know About You
  Though actually written by Berlin, this number
  was credited to Joseph H. McKeon, Harry M.
  Piano, and W. Raymond Walker.
Sadie Salome (Go Home)
  (lyrics by Edgar Leslie)
  Bob Roberts, Columbia A789 (78)
That Mesmerizing Mendelssohn Tune
  (melody based on Felix Mendelssohn's "Spring
  Song")
  Arthur Collins and Byron G. Harlan, Victor
  16472 (78)
  Arthur Collins and Byron G. Harlan, Columbia
  A801 (78)
We'll Wait, Wait, Wait
  (lyrics by Edgar Leslie)

<u>melodies to all following Irving Berlin</u>
<u>lyrics by Ted Snyder</u>:

Christmas Time Seems Years And Years Away
Do Your Duty, Doctor
Good-Bye, Girlie, And Remember Me
I Didn't Go Home At All
If I Thought You Wouldn't Tell
I Just Came Back To Say Good-Bye
I Wish That You Was My Gal, Molly

My Wife's Gone To The Country (Hurrah! Hurrah!)
  Lyrics co-authored by George Whiting, whose wife
  divorced him as a result of this song. (Eighteen
  years later, as atonement for such an aspersion
  on marriage, he wrote "My Blue Heaven".) Two
  hundred additional choruses were written by
  Irving Berlin on special commission of the New
  York Evening Journal, in which all were printed.
  Arthur Collins and Byron G. Harlan, Columbia
  A724 (78)
  Victor Mixed Chorus (medley), Victor 35550
  (12") (78)
Next To Your Mother, Who Do You Love?
  Sung at Carey Walsh's saloon, Coney Island, by
  up-and-coming Eddie Cantor.
No One Could Do It Like My Father
Oh! Where Is My Wife To-Night?
Some Little Something About You
Someone's Waiting For Me
Wild Cherries
  An earlier piano solo by Ted Snyder to which
  lyrics were added by Irving Berlin.
  Victor Orchestra (conducted by Walter B. Rogers),
  Victor 16472 (78)
Oh! How That German Could Love
  Introduced in show "The Girl And The Wizard" by
  Sam Bernard, who is sometimes credited as co-
  lyricist. When Berlin was signed to record his
  present and future compositions for Columbia,
  this turned out to be the first and - unfortu-
  nately - the last one that he recorded.
  Irving Berlin, Columbia A804 (78)

<u>1910:</u>

Before I Go And Marry (I Will Have a Talk With You)

9

Call Me Up Some Rainy Afternoon
   Ada Jones (with American Quartette), Victor
   16508 (78)
   Ada Jones (with Male Chorus), Columbia A855
   (78)
How Can You Love Such A Man?
   Josie Sadler, Edison 10420 (cylinder)
Innocent Bessie Brown
Stop! Stop! Stop! (Love Me Some More)
   (title sometimes incorrectly given as "Stop!
   Stop! Stop! (You're Breaking My Heart)")
   Cloverleaf Four, Lincoln 515 (78)
   Treasury 802 (33-1/3)
   Elida Morris, Victor 16687 (78)
Telling Lies
   (written in collaboration with Henrietta Blank
   and Fred E. Belcher)
Yiddisha Eyes
Yiddle On Your Fiddle (Play Some Ragtime)
   Sung by Fannie Brice in 1936 film "The Great
   Ziegfeld".

   following two numbers introduced by Fannie Brice
         in Ziegfeld show "Follies Of 1910":

The Dance Of The Grizzly Bear
   (better known as "Doing The Grizzly Bear")
   (melody by George Botsford)
   Also sung by Maude Raymond. Featured in 1934
   film "Wharf Angel".
   Teresa Brewer, London 794 (78)
   Billy Murray (with American Quartette), Victor
   16681 (78)
   Sophie Tucker, Mercury MG-20035 (33-1/3)
Good-Bye Becky Cohen

melodies to all following Irving Berlin lyrics by Ted Snyder:

Alexander And His Clarinet
   This was a clarinet solo by Ted Snyder to which
   lyrics were added by Irving Berlin. Neither the
   words nor music had a thing to do with "Alex-
   ander's Ragtime Band".
   Arthur Collins and Byron G. Harlan, Columbia
   A831 (78)
Angels
Colored Romeo
Dat Draggy Rag
Dear Mayme, I Love You
Dreams, Just Dreams
I Love You More Each Day
I'm A Happy Married Man
I'm Going On A Long Vacation
Is There Anything Else That I Can Do For You?
   Ada Jones, Columbia A909 (78)
Piano Man
   Featured in vaudeville, more than forty years
   later, by Gus Van.
Someone Just Like You, Dear
When I Hear You Play That Piano, Bill
   (title sometimes incorrectly given as "Try It On
   Your Piano, Bill")

following numbers interpolated in various Broadway shows:

Bring Back My Lena To Me
   Introduced by Sam Bernard in show "He Came
   From Milwaukee".
   Maurice Burkhardt, Victor 16994 (78)

That Opera Rag
  Introduced by May Irwin in show "Getting A
  Polish".
Herman, Let's Dance That Beautiful Waltz
Wishing
  Above two selections featured in show "Two
  Men And A Girl".
Angelo
It Can't Be Did
Thank You, Kind Sir, Said She
  Above three selections featured in show "Jump-
  ing Jupiter".

   following three numbers featured in Bayes &
     Norworth show "The Jolly Bachelors":

Stop That Rag (Keep On Playing, Honey)
  Introduced by Nora Bayes
If The Managers Only Thought The Same As Mother
Sweet Marie - Make a Rag-A-Time Dance With Me

     following two numbers featured in show
          "Up And Down Broadway":

Sweet Italian Love
That Beautiful Rag
  Both selections introduced and performed in
  show by Irving Berlin (vocal) and Ted Snyder
  (piano), sporting collegiate sweaters and
  tennis racquets. (The original sheet music
  does not credit Snyder as co-author - although
  it credits Sam S. Shubert as the show's co-
  producer [with his brother Lee] when he'd
  been dead five years!)

The Dance of the Grizzly
   Bear   (a)
That Mesmerizing Mendel-   TWO STEP MEDLEY No. 10
   ssohn Tune   (b) Victor Dance Orch-
Sweet Italian Love   (c) estra, Victor
Stop! Stop! Stop! (Love   35190 (12") (78)
   Me Some More)   (d)

1911:

Alexander's Ragtime Band
   Introduced by Irving Berlin at Friars' Frolic
   Of 1911. First performed publicly, in Chicago,
   by female baritone Emma Carus. Simultaneously
   sung with Lew Dockstader's Minstrels by Al
   Jolson, in vaudeville by Eddie Miller and Helen
   Vincent, soon by just about everybody every-
   where. For revivals of this and other Irving
   Berlin songs in films with all-Berlin scores,
   see each film under its year of release.
   Al Jolson, Decca DL-9063 (33-1/3)
   British Brunswick OE-9406 (45) (ep)
   Al Jolson and Bing Crosby (March 25, 1947),
   Decca 40038 (78) *
   Al Jolson and Bing Crosby (May 7, 1947)
   (medley), V-Disc 814 (12") (78)
   Eddie Cantor introducing Bing Crosby and Connee
   Boswell, Decca 1887 / 25495 (78)
   Julie Andrews, Columbia CL-1886 (33-1/3)
   Andrews Sisters, Decca 2442 (78)
   Decca DL-5264 (33-1/3)
   Boswell Sisters, British Parlophone R2562 (78)
   Norman Brooks, Verve MGV-2091 (12") / British
   Decca DLP-1192 (10") (33-1/3)
   Arthur Collins and Byron G. Harlan, Victor 16908
   (78)

13

Arthur Collins and Byron G. Harlan, Columbia
A1032 (78)
Noel Coward (medley), British HMV C.2431 (12")
(78)
Decca Band, Decca 4119 (78)
Alice Faye, Reprise R-6029 (33-1/3)
Benny Goodman Orchestra, Victor 25455 (78)
RCA Victor 47-2954 (45)
Neil Hefti Orchestra, Columbia CL-1516 (33-1/3)
Hoosier Hot Shots, Columbia 20292 (78)
Bunk Johnson's New Orleans Band, Decca 25132 (78)
Ted Lewis (vocal) and his Band, Columbia 1084-D
(78); Columbia CL-2228 [Album C3L35] (33-1/3)
Grady Martin and his Slew Foot Five, Decca 29213
(78)
Clayton McMichens' Georgia Wildcats, Decca 46072
(78)
Johnny Mercer (with Pied Pipers), Capitol 10064
[Album CD-36] (78)
Ethel Merman and Dan Dailey, Donald O'Connor,
Mitzi Gaynor, Johnnie Ray (soundtrack) with 20th
Century Fox Chorus and Orchestra, Decca 90058
(Part 1) - 90057 (Concluded) (12") (78)
Ethel Merman, Decca DL-8178 [Album DX-153]
(33-1/3)
Russ Morgan Orchestra, Decca 28249 (78)
Red Nichols (trumpet) with Miff Mole and The
Little Molers, Columbia 36280 (78)
Kid Ory's Creole Band, Decca 25133 (78)
Prince's Band, Columbia A1126 (78)
Johnnie Ray, Columbia 40391 (78); Columbia
B-2595 (45) (ep); Columbia CL-1227 (33-1/3)
Irene Reid, MGM E4240 (33-1/3)
Bessie Smith, Columbia 14219-D / Columbia 3173-D
[Album C-8] (78)
Joe Venuti (violin), Tempo 410 (78)

Victor Mixed Chorus (medley), Victor 31848 (12")
   (78)
Mark Warnow Orchestra, V-Disc 35 (12") (78)
After the Honeymoon
   (melody by Ted Snyder)
   Walter Van Brunt, Columbia A1073 (78)
Bring Back My Lovin' Man
Bring Me A Ring In The Spring
Business Is Business, Rosey Cohen
Cuddle Up
Dat's-A My Gal
Don't Put Out The Light
   (lyrics by Edgar Leslie)
Down To The Follies Bergere
   (lyrics co-authored by Vincent Bryan; melody co-
   composed by Ted Snyder)
Dying Rag
Everybody's Doing It Now
 Julie Andrews, Columbia CL-1886 (33-1/3)
   Arthur Collins and Byron G. Harlan, Victor 17020
   (78)
   Columbia Quartette, Columbia A1123 (78)
   Ann Southern, Tops L1611 (33-1/3)
He Promised Me
How Do You Do It, Mabel, On Twenty Dollars A Week?
Kiss Me, My Honey, Kiss Me
   (melody by Ted Snyder)
   Featured in 1953 film biography of Eva Tanguay
   "The 'I Don't Care' Girl".
   Elida Morris, Victor 16807 (78)
   Elida Morris, Columbia A906 (78)
   Victor Mixed Chorus (medley), Victor 31848 (12")
   (78)
Meet Me To-Night
Molly O! Oh, Molly
My Melody Dream

One O'Clock In The Morning
  (melody by Ted Snyder)
  Walter Van Brunt, Columbia A1098 (78)
The Ragtime Violin
  Featured in vaudeville (with Bendini & Arthur)
  by Eddie Cantor.
  American Quartette, Victor 17025 (78)
Real Girl
Run Home And Tell Your Mother
  Molly Ames (with Columbia Quartette), Columbia
  A1042 (78)
Sombrero Land
  (lyrics by E. Ray Goetz)
That Kazzatsky Dance
That Monkey Tune
Virginia Lou
What Am I Gonna Do?
  An unpublished number written by Berlin to open
  his act at the Friars' Frolic of 1911.
When I'm Alone I'm Lonesome
  American Quartette, Victor 16884 (78)
  Victor Mixed Chorus (medley), Victor 31848
  (12") (78)
When It Rains, Sweetheart, When It Rains
When You Kiss An Italian Girl
  Maurice Burkhardt, Lksd 70319 (78)
When You're In Town
  Henry Burr and Elise Stevenson, Victor 16898 (78)
  Henry Burr and Elise Stevenson, Columbia A1021
  (78)
  Victor Mixed Chorus (medley), Victor 31848 (12")
  (78)
Whistling Rag
Yankee Love
  (lyrics by E. Ray Goetz)
Yiddisha Nightingale

You've Got Me Hypnotized

<u>following numbers interpolated in</u>
<u>various Broadway shows:</u>

Don't Take Your Beau To The Seashore
(lyrics by E. Ray Goetz)
Featured in show "The Fascinating Widow".
There's A Girl In Havana
Though actually written by Berlin, this number
was credited to E. Ray Goetz and A. Baldwin
Sloane. Featured in show "The Never Homes".
Lyric Quartette, Victor 16985 (78)

<u>following four numbers featured in show</u>
<u>"Temptations" at Follies Bergere Theatre:</u>

Answer Me
Also featured in show "Gaby" (on a double bill
with "Hell").
I Beg Your Pardon, Dear Old Broadway
(lyrics co-authored by Vincent Bryan; melody co-
composed by Ted Snyder)
Also featured in show "Gaby" (on a double bill
with "Hell").
Spanish Love
(lyrics co-authored by Vincent Bryan; melody co-
composed by Ted Snyder)
Andrea Sarto (with Male Chorus), Columbia A1031
(78)
Keep a Taxi Waiting, Dear

<u>following four selections featured in Ziegfeld</u>
<u>shows "Jardin De Paris", on roof of Amsterdam</u>
<u>Theatre, and (shortly) "Ziegfeld Follies Of</u>
<u>1911", in theatre itself:</u>

17

Woodman, Woodman, Spare That Tree
(written in collaboration with Vincent Bryan)
Sung and immortalized by Bert Williams
Phil Harris, Vocalion 3466 / Okeh 6325 (78)
Phil Harris, ARA 153 (78)
Phil Harris, RCA Victor 20-2683 (78); RCA Victor
47-2720 (45)
Bob Roberts, Victor 16909 (78)
Bert Williams, Columbia A1321 (78)
Doggone That Chilly Man
Ephraham Played Upon The Piano
(written in collaboration with Vincent Bryan)
Sung by the great Bert Williams
You've Built A Fire Down In My Heart
Also featured in show "The Fascinating Widow"
(see above).

Take A Little Tip From Father	(a)	TWO-STEP MEDLEY,
The Ragtime Violin	(b)	Arthur Pryor's
I Want To Be In Dixie	(c)	Band, Victor
Everybody's Doing It Now	(d)	17091 (78)

1912:

Antonio, You'd Better Come Home
At The Devil's Ball
Peerless Quartette, Victor 17315 (78)
Becky's Got A Job In A Musical Show
Belle Of The Barbers' Ball
(melody by George M. Cohan, with the exception
of a brief excerpt from Berlin's 1910 "Yiddle
On Your Fiddle")
Call Again
Come Back To Me - My Melody
(melody by Ted Snyder)

18

Do It Again
Don't Leave Your Wife Alone
Down In My Heart
Elevator Man (Going Up – Going Up – Going Up)
Father's Beard
Fiddle Dee Dee
    (also known as "He Played It On His Fid-Fid-
    Fiddle Dee Dee")
    (lyrics by E. Ray Goetz
    Introduced by Lew Dockstader.
    Lew Dockstader (with Male Quartette), Columbia
    A1200 (78); Audio LPA-2285 (33-1/3)
    Walter Van Brunt and Maurice Burkhardt, Victor
    17150 (78)
The Funny Little Melody
    Walter Van Brunt and Maurice Burkhardt, Victor
    17213 (78)
Goody Goody Goody Goody Goody Good
Hiram's Band
    Though actually written by Berlin, this number
    was credited to E. Ray Goetz and A. Baldwin
    Sloane.
I'm Afraid, Pretty Maid, I'm Afraid
    Ada Jones and Walter Van Brunt, Columbia A1164
    (78)
I've Got To Have Some Lovin' Now
Keep Away From The Fellow Who Owns An Automobile
Lead Me To That Beautiful Band
    (lyrics by E. Ray Goetz)
    Introduced by Happy Lambert with Cohan & Harris
    Minstrels.
My Sweet Italian Man
Pick, Pick, Pick, Pick On The Mandolin, Antonio
Ragtime Mocking Bird
    Dolly Connolly, Columbia A1126 (78)

Ragtime Soldier Man
  Arthur Collins and Byron G. Harlan, Victor
  17150 (78)
Spring And Fall
Take A Little Tip From Father
  (melody by Ted Snyder)
  Don Meehan, Folkways FS-3858 (33-1/3)
  Billy Murray, Victor 17064 (78)
That Mysterious Rag
  (melody by Ted Snyder)
  American Quartette, Victor 16982 (78)
That's How I Love You
True Born Soldier Man
Wait Until Your Daddy Comes Home
When I Lost You
  This was written for Berlin's bride, Dorothy
  Goetz (E. Ray's sister), on her death follow-
  ing their honeymoon in Cuba. It was his first
  ballad hit.
  Buffalo Bills (male quartette), Decca 27696 (78);
  Decca DL-5361 (33-1/3)
  Henry Burr, Victor 17275 (78)
  Bing Crosby (Decca) 3477 / 25093 / 25187 (78)
  Jimmy Durante, Warner Bros. W1577 (33-1/3)
  Frank Froeba (piano), Decca 24235 [Album A-609]
  (78); Decca DL-5048 (33-1/3)
  Arthur Godfrey, Columbia 38303 (78)
  Frank Sinatra, Reprise F-1007 (33-1/3)
  Kate Smith, MGM 10220 (78)
  Jayne Walton, Mercury 5002 (78)
When I'm Thinking Of You
When Johnson's Quartette Harmonize
When The Midnight Choo-Choo Leaves For Alabam'
  Norman Brooks, Promenade 2107 / Piourette FM-3 /
  Coronet CX-45 (33-1/3)

Arthur Collins and Byron G. Harlan, Victor
17246 (78)
Arthur Collins and Byron G. Harlan, Columbia
A1246 (78)
Jack LaDelle, Design DLP-107 (33-1/3)
Ethel Merman and Dan Dailey, Decca 90057
(12") (78)
Yiddisha Professor

<u>following numbers interpolated in
various Broadway shows</u>:

Little Bit Of Everything
    Featured in show "Ziegfeld Follies Of 1912".
Follow Me Around
    Featured in show "My Best Girl".
Ragtime Jockey Man
    Featured in show "The Passing Show Of 1912".
Million Dollar Ball
    (lyrics by E. Ray Goetz)
    Featured in show "Hanky Panky".
Alexander's Bagpipe Band
    (lyrics co-authored by E. Ray Goetz; melody co-
    composed by A. Baldwin Sloane)
    Introduced by Fay Templeton in Weber & Fields
    show "Hokey Pokey".
    Billy Murray, Victor 17054 (78)

<u>following three numbers featured in Al Jolson
show "The Whirl of Society"</u>:

That Society Bear
    Sung by Stella Mayhew
    Walter Van Brunt, Victor 17068 (78)
I Want To Be In Dixie
    (title sometimes incorrectly given as "I'm Going

21

Back to Dixie Land" or "I'm Going Back to Dixie")
(melody by Ted Snyder)
Sung by Courtenay Sisters.
Arthur Collins and Byron G. Harlan, Victor
17075 (78)
Arthur Collins and Byron G. Harlan, Silvertone
19679 (78)
Gene Greene, Pathe 536 (90)
Ragtime Sextette
Sung by Al Jolson (lead) with Jose Collins,
Edward Cutler, Ernest Hare, Stella Mayhew,
Cecil Ryan, and Billee Taylor. This was a rag-
time parody arrangement of Donizetti's "Chi Mi
Frena?" from the opera "Luci di Lammermoor",
shortly also featured in show "Hanky Panky" (see
above) under title "Lucia Sextette Burlesque".
Billy Murray (with Vaudeville Quartette),
Victor 17119 (78)

When The Midnight Choo-Choo	
Leaves for Alabam'	(a)
When I Lost You	(b) SONG MEDLEY No. 6
Snookey Ookums	(c) "SNYDER SPECIALS",
*Take Me Back To The Garden	Victor Mixed Chorus
of Love	(d) Victor 35305 (12")
At The Devil's Ball	(e) (78)

When The Midnight Choo-Choo	
Leaves for Alabam'	(a) MEDLEY, Victor
*The Ghost Of The Violin	(b) Military Band,
Welcome Home	(c) Victor 35277 (12")
At The Devil's Ball	(d) (78)

*not by Berlin

Abie Sings An Irish Song
Anna 'Lize's Wedding Day
The Apple Tree And The Bumble Bee
Daddy Come Home
  Billy Murray, Victor 17519 (78)
Down In Chattanooga
  Arthur Collins and Byron G. Harlan, Victor
  17527 (78)
Happy Little Country Girl
  Elida Morris, Victor 17430 (78)
He's So Good To Me
If All The Girls I Knew Were Like You
If You Don't Want Me Why Do You Hang Around?
In My Harem
  An anonymous parody, "In The Army" was sung with
  great zest and often unprintable lyrics by the
  Doughboys of World War I.
  Walter Van Brunt, Columbia A1302 (78)
I Was Aviating Around
  (title sometimes incorrectly given as "I Was
  Waiting Around")
The International Rag
  Irving Berlin wrote this number while crossing
  the Atlantic, and introduced it on a triumphal
  vaudeville tour of England.
  Arthur Collins and Byron G. Harlan, Victor
  17431 (78)
Jake - Jake
Keep On Walking
Kiss Your Sailor Boy Good-Bye
The Ki-Yi-Yodeling Dog
Monkey Doodle Doo

The Old Maid's Ball
  Arthur Collins and Byron G. Harlan, Columbia
  A1345 (78)
Pullman Porters' Parade
  (lyrics by Irving Berlin under the pseudonym
  "Ren G. May"; melody by Maurice Abrahams)
  Al Jolson, Columbia A1374 (78)
  Will Halley, Victor 17453 (78)
Rum Tum Tiddle
San Francisco Bound
Snookey Ookums
  Joe ("Fingers") Carr (piano), Capitol 1074 (78)
  Frankie Froeba (piano), Decca 27142 (78)
  Billy Murray, Victor 17313 (78)
  Cliff Stewart and The San Francisco Boys,
  Coral 60292 (78)
Take Me Back
  Henry Burr, Victor 17507 (78)
There's A Girl In Arizona
  (written in collaboration with Grant Clarke
  and Edgar Leslie)
They've Got Me Doin' It Now
  This number consisted mostly of excerpts from
  every ragtime hit Berlin ever wrote.
  Billy Murray, Victor 17429 (78)
Tra, La! La! La!
  Arthur Collins and Byron G. Harlan, Victor
  17481 (78)
We Have Much To Be Thankful For
Welcome Home
  Peerless Quartette, Victor 17322 (78)
You Picked A Bad Day Out To Say Good-Bye
You've Got Your Mother's Big Blue Eyes
  Introduced by Al Jolson
  Lillian Davis, Victor 17482 (78)

following numbers interpolated in
various Broadway shows:

At The Picture Show
  Though actually written by Berlin, this number
  was credited to E. Ray Goetz and A. Baldwin
  Sloane. Featured in show "The Sun Dodgers".
Somebody's Coming To My House
  Featured in show "All Aboard". Sung some years
  later by Oliver Hardy in a Laurel and Hardy
  two-reel comedy (title unknown).
  Walter Van Brunt, Victor 17381 (78)

In My Harem	(a) Medley One-Step,
Wait Until Your Daddy Comes	(b) Victor Military
Home	Band, Victor
Snookey Ookums	(c) 17325 (78)

Snookey Ookums	(a) MEDLEY ONE-STEP,
The Old Maid's Ball	(b) Victor Military
There's A Girl in Havana	(c) Band, Victor
	17375 (78)

Somebody's Coming To My	
House	(a) MEDLEY TWO-STEP,
Happy Little Country Girl	(b) Victor Military
You've Got Your Mother's	Band, Victor
Big Blue Eyes	(c) 35322 (12") (78)

Down In Chattanooga	(a) ACCORDION MEDLEY,
Kiss Your Sailor Boy Good-	Pietro Deiro,
Bye	(b) Victor 17574 (78)

25

The following Irving Berlin Medley is preceded by
Maxim's Cabaret Singers (an all-girl chorus) singing the same Spanish song of which Al Jolson renders
part on his January 8, 1920, recording of "That
Wonderful Kid From Madrid" (Columbia A2898) and
plays on the piano for Ruby Keeler's dance audition
in "Go Into Your Dance" (Warner Bros., 1935). I
don't know the title and I'm not sure the following male vocalist is Will Halley, but it sounds
like him. During the girl's vocals, he's also
heard hollering and carrying on in the background. The record ends with his being thrown
out.

When I Lost You (MAXIM'S CABARET SINGERS)	(a)	
Down In Chattanooga (WILL HALLEY AND MAXIM'S CABARET SINGERS)	(b)	NIGHT SCENE IN MAXIM'S, Columbia A1509 (78)
The International Rag (MAXIM'S CABARET SINGERS)	(c)	

1914:

Along Came Ruth
   (title taken from that of a play then running
   on Broadway)
   During 1926, a special parody saluting Babe
   Ruth was written by Christy Walsh, Addy Britt,
   and Harry Link.
   Fred Astaire (medley), Kapp KL-1165 (33-1/3)
   Arthur Fields, Victor 17637 (78)
Always Treat Her Like A Baby
   Irving Kaufman, Victor 17636 (78)
Come To The Land Of The Argentine
Furnishing A Home For Two

26

God Gave You To Me
Haunted House
He's A Devil In His Own Home Town
 (lyrics co-authored by Grant Clarke)
 Kay Kyser Orchestra (vocal by Marwyn Bogue),
 Brunswick 7555 (78)
 Ed Morton, Columbia A1525 (78)
 Billy Murray, Victor 17576 (78)
 Benay Venuta, Mercury MG-25006 (33-1/3)
He's A Rag Picker
 Peerless Quartette, Victor 17655 (78)
 Peerless Quartette, Columbia A1628 (78)
If I Had You
If That's Your Idea Of A Wonderful Time (Take
 Me Home)
 Ada Jones, Victor 17630 (78)
If You Don't Want My Peaches You Better Stop
 Shaking My Tree
I Hate You
I Love To Quarrel With You
 Featured in vaudeville by Fred and Adele
 Astaire.
 Fred Astaire (medley), Kapp KL-1165 (33-1/3)
It Isn't What He Said (It's The Way He Said It)
I Want To Go Back To Michigan (Down On The
 Farm)
 Morton Harvey, Victor 17650 (78)
Morning Exercise
Revival Day
 Al Jolson, Columbia A1621 (78)
Stay Down Here Where You Belong
 A splendid pacifist number which Berlin seems
 to consider the worst song he ever wrote. At
 parties, Groucho Marx will sing and play it
 just to annoy him.
 Henry Burr, Victor 17716 (78)

27

Arthur Fields, Columbia A1628 (78)
That's My Idea Of Paradise
They're On Their Way To Mexico
   Heidelberg Quintette (starring Will Oakland),
   Victor 17599 (78)
   Victor Military Band, Victor 17592 (78)
This Is The Life
   Introduced by Al Jolson
   Pietro Deiro (accordion medley), Victor
   17574 (78)
   Nappy LeMar's Strawhat Seven, Capitol 1047
   (78)
   Billy Murray, Victor 17584 (78)
   Peerless Quartette, Columbia A1509 (78)
When It's Night-Time In Dixieland
   Will Halley (I think!), Little Wonder Record
   No. 137 (5-1/2") (78)
Follow The Crowd
   Interpolated in show "Queen Of The Movies".

On December 8, 1914, Charles B. Dillingham
presented the first stage musical with a complete
score by Irving Berlin: "Watch Your Step".
Starred were Vernon & Irene Castle, making their
Broadway debut, with Elizabeth Brice and Charles
King, Sallie Fisher, Frank Tinney, Elizabeth
Murray, Harry Kelly, and Justine Johnstone.
Berlin score:

Chatter, Chatter
I Love To Have The Boys Around Me
I've Gotta Go Back To Texas
Lead Me To Love
Let's Go Around The Town
Lock Me In Your Harem And Throw Away The Key
Look At Them Doing It!

28

Metropolitan Nights
Minstrel Parade
    Sung by Elizabeth Murray.
    Arthur Collins and Byron G. Harlan, Victor
    17783 (78)
Move Over
Office Hours
Opera Burlesque
    This was one of the most complicated popular
    production numbers ever scored, requiring seven-
    teen pages of sheet music.
Play A Simple Melody
    Sung as possibly the first counter-melody duet
    by Sallie Fisher and Charles King.
    Bing and Gary Crosby, Decca 27112 (78)*; Decca
    ED-2001 (45) (ep)
    Georgia Gibbs, Coral 60227 (78)
    Phil Harris, RCA Victor 20-3781 (78)
    Johnny Maddox (piano), Dot 15325 (78)
    Ethel Merman and Dan Dailey, Decca 29379 (10")/
    Decca 90057 (12")(78)
    Billy Murray and Edna Brown, Victor 18051 (78)
    Jean Sablon, RCA Victor 20-3537 (78); RCA Victor
    47-3026 (45)
    Dinah Shore, Columbia 38837 (78)
    Jo Stafford, Capitol 1039 (78)
Settle Down In A One-Horse Town
    Billy Murray and Ada Jones, Victor 17708 (78)
Show Me How To Do The Fox Trot
Syncopated Walk
    Sung and danced by Vernon and Irene Castle.
    Peerless Quartette, Victor 17748 (78)
They Always Follow Me Around
Watch Your Step
What Is Love?
When I Discovered You

When I Discovered You   (a) "WATCH YOUR STEP"
I Love To Have The Boys   MEDLEY ONE-STEP,
    Around Me   (b) Victor Military Band
                                   Victor 17727 (10")
                                   (78)

Syncopated Walk   (a) "WATCH YOUR STEP"
Settle Down In A One-   MEDLEY FOX TROT,
    Horse Town   (b) Victor Military Band
                                   Victor 35432 (12")
                                   (78)

1915:

Araby
    Featured in vaudeville by Eddie Cantor.
    Harry Macdonough, Victor 17889 (78)
Cohen Owes Me Ninety-Seven Dollars
    Rhoda Bernard, Victor 18023 (78)
Homeward Bound
I Love To Stay At Home
    Billy Murray, Victor 17855 (78)
I'm Going Back To The Farm
My Bird Of Paradise
    Charlie Tobias, Eddie Cantor's cousin-in-law
    and staunchest imitator, won his first amateur
    contest singing a parody on this song which he
    wrote himself.
    Hilo Orchestra, Victor 21424 (78)
    Louise and Ferera (Hawaiian guitars), Victor
    17892 (78)
    Peerless Quartette, Victor 17770 (78)
Once In May
Sailor Song

30

Si's Been Drinking Cider
  Arthur Collins and Byron G. Harlan, Columbia
  A1754 (78)
Until I Fell In Love With You
Voice Of Belgium
When I Leave The World Behind
  (lyrics suggested by the legacy of Charles
  Lounsbury, to whom this song was dedicated)
  Introduced by Al Jolson. A particular Jolson
  favorite of Charlie Chaplin's.
  Al Jolson, Decca 24399 (78); Decca DL-5030 (10")/
  Decca DL-9034 (12") (33-1/3)
  Sam Ash, Columbia A1772 (78)
  Teresa Brewer, Coral CRL-57027 (33-1/3)
  Norman Brooks, Promenade 2107/Piourette FM-3/
  Coronet CX-45 (33-1/3)
  Henry Burr, Victor 17874 (78)
When You're Down in Louisville (Call On Me)
  Anna Chandler, Columbia A1939 (78)
  Arthur Collins and Byron G. Harlan, Victor
  17955 (78)
While The Band Played An American Rag

Berlin's second revue, again presented by Dillingham, was "Stop! Look! Listen!". Gaby Deslys
starred with Harry Pilcer, Blossom Seeley,
Marion Harris, Doyle and Dixon, Tempest and Sunshine, Harry Fox, Frank Lalor, and Joseph Santly.
Berlin score:

And Father Wanted Me To Learn A Trade
Blow Your Horn
Everything In America Is Ragtime
  (also known as "Ragtime Finale")
  Sung by Gaby Deslys.

Give Us A Chance
   (also known as "Why Don't They Give Us A Chance?")
The Girl On The Magazine Cover
   "Cover girls" in this production number included
   Justine Johnstone, Helen Barnes, Evelyn Conway,
   Eleanor St. Claire, Hazel Lewis, and Marion
   Davies. Years later, Miss Davies restaged the
   number at one of her birthday parties in the
   Hearst castle.
   Fred Astaire (medley), Kapp KL-1165 (33-1/3)
   Harry Macdonough (with Victor Mixed Chorus),
   Victor 17945 (78)
I Love A Piano
   Of all the songs he ever wrote, this is Mr.
   Berlin's favorite.
   Arthur Collins and Byron G. Harlan, Little
   Wonder Record No. 403 (5-1/2") (78)
   Billy Murray, Victor 17945 (78)
   Blossom Seeley, Mercury 71071 (45); Mercury
   MG-20224 (33-1/3)
I Love To Dance
I'm Coming Home With A Skate On
The Law Must Be Obeyed
A Pair Of Ordinary Coons
Stop! Look! Listen!
Take Off A Little Bit
Teach Me How To Love
That Hula Hula
   Harry Macdonough, Victor 17930 (78)
When I Get Back To The U.S.A.
   Sung as a counter-melody to Henry Carey's
   "America (My Country 'Tis Of Thee)".
   Billy Murray (with Victor Mixed Chorus),
   Victor 17930 (78)
When I'm Out With You

I Love A Piano	(a)	"STOP! LOOK! LISTEN!"
That Hula Hula	(b)	MEDLEY FOX TROT, Victor
The Girl On The		Military Band, Victor
Magazine Cover	(c)	35521 (12") (78)
When I Get Back To		
The U.S.A.	(d)	

1916:

By The Sad Luana Shore
Friars' Parade
He's Getting Too Darn Big For A One-Horse Town
Hurry Back To My Bamboo Shack
In Florida Among The Palms
  Irving Kaufman, Columbia A2091 (78)
  Sterling Trio, Victor 18138 (78)
I'm Down In Honolulu Looking Them Over
  Al Jolson, Columbia A2143 (78) [Jolson's rarest
  record - discontinued immediately on release!]
I'm Not Prepared
Just Give Me Ragtime Please
Someone Else May Be There While I'm Gone
  Introduced by Al Jolson
  Al Jolson (1916), Columbia A2124 (78)
  Al Jolson (1947), Decca 24398 (78); Decca
  DL-5030 (10")/DL-9035 (12") (33-1/3)
When The Black Sheep Returns To The Fold
  Avon Comedy Four, Victor 18126 (78)
You Ought To Go To Paris

following three numbers featured in show "Step This Way":

I've Got A Sweet Tooth Bothering Me
  M. J. O'Connell, Victor 18073 (78)

33

When You Drop Off At Cairo, Illinois
  Billy Murray, Victor 18102 (78)
Step This Way

Irving Berlin and Victor Herbert each wrote about half the songs for "The Century Girl". This Ziegfeld revue featured Elsie Janis, Van and Schenck, Doyle and Dixon, Sam Bernard, Hazel Dawn, Maurice, Lillian Tashman, Florence Walton, Irving Fisher, Leon Errol, John Slavin, and Frank Tinney. Berlin wrote a ragtime counter-melody to Herbert's "Kiss Me Again", plus the following selections:

Alice In Wonderland
  Harry Macdonough and Anna Howard, Victor 18211
  (78)
It Takes An Irishman To Make Love
The Music Lesson
On The Train Of A Wedding Gown
That Broadway Chicken Walk
You've Got Me Doing It Too

		"CENTURY GIRL" MEDLEY
That Broadway Chicken Walk	(a)	FOX TROT, Victor
Alice In Wonderland	(b)	Military Band, Victor 18218 (78)

1917:

For Your Country And My Country
  Frances Alda, Victor 64689 (78)
  Willie Weston, Victor 18307 (78)
From Here To Shanghai
  Introduced by Al Jolson
  Al Jolson, Columbia A2224 (78)

34

Gene Greene (with Peerless Quartette), Victor
    18242 (78)
How Can I Forget (When There's So Much To Remember)
    Robert Lewis, Columbia A2287 (78)
    Alan Turner, Victor 18352 (78)
Let's All Be Americans Now
    (lyrics co-authored by Edgar Leslie; melody co-
    composed by George W. Meyer)
    American Quartette, Victor 18256 (78)
    Knickerbocker Quartette, Columbia A2225 (78)
Mr. Jazz Himself
My Sweetie
    Joseph C. Smith's Orchestra, Victor 18407 (78)
Poor Little Cinderella
Pretty Birdie
Put A Little Letter In My Letter Box
The Road That Leads To Love
Smile And Show Your Dimple
    Sam Ash, Columbia A2425 (78)
That Goody Melody
    Irving Kaufman, Columbia A2184 (78)
There Are Two Eyes In Dixie
There's Something Nice About The South
    Gus Van and Joe Schenck, Victor 18269 (78)
Wasn't It Yesterday
Whose Little Heart Are You Breaking Now?
    Albert Campbell and Henry Burr, Victor 18378
    (78)

        following numbers interpolated in
            various Broadway shows:

I'll Take You Back To Italy
    Featured in Fred Stone show "Jack O' Lantern".
    Billy Murray and Ada Jones, Victor 18436 (78)
Poor Little Rich Girl's Dog

35

Featured in Julia Sanderson show "Rambler Rose".

For Your Country And My Country	(a)	MEDLEY, Conway's Band, Victor
Let's All Be Americans Now	(b)	18345 (78)

Irving Berlin and George M. Cohan each wrote about half the songs for "Cohan Revue Of 1918". (In "Hello, Broadway!", 1914, Cohan had written and introduced "Those Irving Berlin Melodies", a production number interpolating snatches of "The International Rag", "Everybody's Doing It Now", "Alexander's Ragtime Band", and others.) Starred was Nora Bayes (at whose request Berlin rewrote some of her material) with Fred Santley, Charles Winninger, and Irving Fisher. Berlin score:

A Bad Chinaman From Shanghai
Down Where The Jack O'Lanterns Grow
King Of Broadway
A Man Is Only A Man
Polly, Pretty Polly (Polly With A Past)
  (melody by George M. Cohan)
Show Me The Way
Wedding Of Words And Music

Another revue for which Irving Berlin wrote about half the songs: "Dance And Grow Thin". Featured were Gus Van and Joe Schenck, Gertrude Hoffman, Leon Errol, Harry Kelly, Joe Jackson, and Irving Fisher. Berlin score:

Birdie
Cinderella Lost Her Slipper

Dance And Grow Thin
   (melody co-authored by George W. Meyer)
   Gus Van and Joe Schenck, Victor 18258 (78)
Letter Boxes
Mary Brown
Way Down South

1918:

The Devil Has Bought Up All The Coal
   Marconi Brothers (accordion trio) (medley),
   Columbia A2565 (78)
Dream On, Little Soldier Boy
   John McCormack made a Victor recording of this
   song which was never released.
Good-Bye, France
   Nora Bayes, Columbia A2678 (78)
I Have Just One Heart For Just One Boy
I Wouldn't Give That For The Boy Who Couldn't
   Dance
Over The Sea, Boys
Send A Lot Of Jazz Bands Over There
Sterling Silver Moon
They Were All Out Of Step But Jim
   Billy DeRex, Gennett 8507 (78)
   Billy Murray, Victor 18465 (78)
   Eddie Nelson, Emerson 932 (78)
   Gus Van and Joe Schenck, Columbia A2630 (78)
When The Curtain Falls
You've Been The Sunshine Of My Life

following numbers interpolated in
various Broadway shows:

Blue Devils Of France

Introduced by Lillian Lorraine in show "Zieg-
feld Follies Of 1918".
I'm Gonna Pin My Medal On The Girl I Left Behind
Me
Introduced by Frank Carter in show "Ziegfeld
Follies Of 1918".
Peerless Quartette, Victor 18486 (78)
The Circus Is Coming To Town
Come Along To Toy Town
Above two selections featured in show "Every-
thing".
It's The Little Bit Of Irish
Featured in Julia Sanderson show "The Canary".

Upon being drafted, Irving Berlin wrote the Army
revue "Yip, Yip, Yaphank". Produced at the Century
Theatre, August 19, 1918, this featured a cast
of 350 doughboys from Camp Upton, Fort Yaphank,
including Privates Hughie L. Clark, James Reilly,
Harry Green, Solly Cutner (in the Minstrel Show
segment), Snyder, Ferrerier, Belles, Loher,
Kendall, Newman, Fitzpatrick, and Sammy Lee;
Peter O'Neill, Peter J. Burns, Dan Healy, Jack
Riano, John Murphy, Harold Kennedy (all of whom
appeared a quarter-century later in Berlin's
"This Is The Army"); Sergeants William Bauman
(as Interlocutor), Benny Leonard (World Light-
weight Champion, in a boxing exhibition with
Private Miglion), and Irving Berlin. Berlin
score:

Mandy
Sung by Private Murphy (with Pickaninnies
and Chorus) to Private Healy (as Mandy).
Bevo

Above two selections reprised in show "Ziegfeld
Follies of 1919". For recordings of the former,
consult same.
Poor Little Me - I'm On KP
(also known as "Kitchen Police")
Oh! How I Hate To Get Up In The Morning
Above two selections introduced in "Yip, Yip,
Yaphank" by Irving Berlin himself. Both re-
vived in 1942 show and 1943 film "This Is The
Army", the latter once again sung by Berlin.
For recordings of same, consult that show.
Berlin's mother saw her son on the stage for
the first time performing these woe-begone
ditties, went home very much put out with the
way the Army seemed to be treating him, and
died shortly after.
Ding Dong
Peerless Quartette, Columbia A2647 (78)
Hello, Hello, Hello
I Can Always Find A Little Sunshine In The Y.M.C.A.
Sung by Private Johnson, to the great derision
of the audience.
Peerless Quartette, Columbia A2647 (78)
Ragtime Razor Brigade
Soldier Boy
What A Difference A Uniform Will Make
(also known as "Ever Since I Put On A Uniform")
We're On Our Way To France
The entire all-soldier cast was suddenly ordered
overseas during the show's 32nd performance.
They marched up the aisles and out of the
theatre singing this song.

1919:

The Hand That Rocked My Cradle Rules My Heart

Henry Burr, Emerson 1074 (78)
John Steel, Victor 18611 (78)
Was There Ever A Pal Like You
Henry Burr, Columbia A2861 (78)

The above two selections were written, following her death, to honor Berlin's mother.

Everything Is Rosy Now For Rosie
  (lyrics co-authored by Grant Clarke)
Eyes Of Youth
I Left My Door Open And My Daddy Walked Out
I Lost My Heart In Dixieland
Harry Fox, Columbia A2828 (78)
I Never Knew
  (lyrics by Elsie Janis)
  Arthur Fields, Emerson 10130 (78)
  George Meader, Columbia A2826 (78)
I've Got My Captain Working For Me Now
  Al Jolson, Columbia A2794 (78); Audio LPA-2285
  (33-1/3)
  Bing Crosby (with Billy DeWolfe), V-Disc 820
  (12")   (78)
  Billy Murray, Victor 18604 (78)
  Billy Murray, Emerson 1042 (78)
I Wonder
The New Moon
Nobody Knows (And Nobody Seems To Care)
  Irving and Jack Kaufman, Columbia A2795 (78)
  Irving and Jack Kaufman, Emerson 10101 (78)
  Esther Walker, Victor 18613 (78)
Since Katy The Waitress Became An Avaitress
Sweeter Than Sugar (Is My Sweetie)
When My Baby Smiles
  Henry Burr, Columbia A2894 (78)

following numbers interpolated in
various Broadway shows:

You're So Beautiful
  Featured in Julia Sanderson show "The Canary".
That Revolutionary Rag
  Featured in George M. Cohan show "The Royal
  Vagabond".

Nobody Knows (And Nobody Seems To Care)	(a)	Rudy Wiedoeft (saxophone), Harry Akst and Carl Fenton (piano), Brunswick 2025 (78)
Sweeter Than Sugar (Is My Sweetie)	(b)	

Nobody Knows (And Nobody Seems To Care)	(a)	Hickman Trio (saxophone and pianos from Art Hickman band), Columbia A2839 (78)
I Lost My Heart In Dixieland	(b)	

Irving Berlin wrote nearly the entire score for
"Ziegfeld Follies of 1919". This greatest of all
Ziegfeld Follies starred Eddie Cantor, Bert Williams, Gus Van and Joe Schenck, Marilyn Miller,
John Steel, Eddie Dowling, DeLyle Alda, Johnny
and Ray Dooley, and the Fairbanks Twins. Berlin
score:

Bevo
Harem Life
I'm The Guy Who Guards The Harem
I Want To See A Minstrel Show
  Introduction to Minstrel Show segment starring
  Bert Williams and Eddie Cantor as end-men.

41

Danny Kaye and Bing Crosby (medley), Decca
29341 [Album A-956] (78)
Look Out For The Bolsheviki Man
Mandy
  Sung by Gus Van and Joe Schenck. Revived by
  Eddie Cantor in 1934 film "Kid Millions"; also
  by Donald O'Connor in a 1944 film of which I
  don't know the title.
  Norman Brooks (1960), Promenade 2238/Parade
  SP-351/Spinorama MK-3051 (33-1/3)
  Norman Brooks (1965), Sure SM-Vol. 23 (33-1/3)
  Eddie Cantor, Melotone 13183/Conqueror 8351/
  Rex 8390 (78)
  Danny Kaye and Bing Crosby (medley), Decca
  29341 [Album A-956] (78)
  Shannon Four, Victor 18605 (78)
  Gus Van and Joe Schenck, Columbia A2780 (78)
My Tambourine Girl
The Near Future
Prohibition
A Pretty Girl Is Like A Melody
  Sung by John Steel while pretty girls permeated
  the stage as melodies "Humoresque" (Mauricette),
  "Spring Song" (Hazel Washburn), "Elegy" (Martha
  Pierre), "Barcarolle" (Jessie Reed), "Serenade"
  (Alta King), and "Traumerei" (Margaret Irving);
  piano played by Lucille Jarrot. Sung by Dennis
  Morgan in 1936 film "The Great Ziegfeld"; re-
  vived in ersatz night club revue "Ziegfeld
  Follies Of 1956", plus being played at more
  burlesque and fashion shows and beauty pagents
  than probably any other song ever written.
  Kenny Backer, Victor 26664 (78)
  Ray Bloch Orchestra, V-Disc 872 (12") (78)
  Sonny Kendis and Stork Club Orchestra, Columbia
  36396 [Album C-75] (78)

42

Grady Martin and his Slew Foot Five, Decca
29328 (78)
Tony Martin, Decca 91777 [Album ED-414] (45)
(ep)
Joe Reichman (piano), Victor 27658 [Album P-91]
(78)
Ethel Smith (console organ), Decca 24321 (78)
Eddie South Orchestra, Columbia 35633 [Album
C-27] (78)
John Steel, Victor 18588 (78)
Alec Templeton (piano), Columbia 36164 (78)
Syncopated Cocktail
We Made The Doughnuts Over There
You Cannot Make Your Shimmy Shake On Tea
  (lyrics co-authored by Rennold Woolf)
  Sung by Bert Williams.
You'd Be Surprised
  Sung by Eddie Cantor. He made it such a hit
  that it was shortly interpolated in shows
  "Shubert Gaieties" (sung by Georgie Jessel) and
  "Oh! What A Girl" (sung by Lew Cooper).
  Eddie Cantor (1919), Emerson 10102 (78)
  Eddie Cantor (1944), Decca 23987 (78); Ace
  of Hearts AH·68 (33-1/3)
  Ada Jones, Paramount 33042 (78)
  Irving Kaufman, Columbia A2815 (78)
  Kathy Linden, Felsted FL-7501 (33-1/3)
  Billy Murray, Victor 18634 (78)
  Billy Murray, Okeh 4042 (78)
  Johnnie Ray, Columbia 40154 (78)
  Orrin Tucker Orchestra (vocal by Wee Bonnie
  Baker), Columbia 35344 (78)

Mandy   (a) Selvin's Novelty Orch-
A Pretty Girl Is Like (b) estra, Victor 18614
  A Melody   (78)

I Want To See A Minstrel (a) Bing Crosby and
   Show   Danny Kaye, (with
Mandy   (b) Chorus), Decca
                        29341 (78)

1920:

After You Get What You Want You Don't Want It
  Dolores Gray, Decca 29380 (10")/Decca 90058
  (12") (78)
  Marilyn Monroe, 20th Fox FXG-5000 (33-1/3)
  Gus Van and Joe Schenck, Columbia A2966 (78)
But She's Just A Little Bit Crazy About Her Husband
  - That's All
Come Again
Drowsy Head
  (written in collaboration with Vaughn DeLeath)
  Orpheus Trio, Actuelle 020552 (78)
Home Again Blues
  (melody by Harry Akst)
  This was written during the time Akst was
  working with Berlin as his "amanuensis".
  He looked it up in the dictionary, found
  it meant "stooge", and quit - to become Al
  Jolson's amanuensis.
  Frank Crumit, Columbia A3375 (78)
  Aileen Stanley, Victor 18760 (78)
I Know Why
Just Another Kill
Lindy
Relatives
A Streak Of Blues

following numbers interpolated in
various Broadway shows:

Beautiful Faces (Need Beautiful Clothes)
    Featured in show "Broadway Brevities of 1920".
    This was to have been revived in the 1947
    Berlin film "Easter Parade", but was instead
    left on the cutting-room floor.
    Paul Whiteman Orchestra, Victor 18737 (78)
Metropolitan Ladies
    Featured in show "Ziegfeld Girls Of 1920"
    (also known as "Ziegfeld's 9 O'Clock Revue").
I'll See You In C-U-B-A
    Featured in show "Ziegfeld Midnight Frolic Of
    1920". Popularized by Ted Lewis.
    Jack Kaufman, Columbia A2898 (78)
    Ted Lewis Jazz Band, Columbia A2927 (78)
    Billy Murray, Victor 18652 (78)
    Billy Murray, Aeolian-Vocalion 14035 (78)
    Three Kaufields (Arthur Fields, Irving and
    Jack Kaufman), Emerson 10158 (78)

As the year before, Irving Berlin wrote nearly
all the songs for "Ziegfeld Follies of 1920".
Starred were Gus Van and Joe Schenck, George
Moran and Charles E. Mack, Mary Eaton, John
Steel, Jack Donahue, Charles Winninger, Ray
Dooley, DeLyle Alda, Carl Randall, Bernard
Granville, Fannie Brice, W.C. Fields, and Art
Hickman and his Orchestra. Berlin score:

Bells
Chinese Firecrackers
Come Along [Sextette]
The Girls Of My Dreams
    Sung by John Steel.
    John Steel, Victor 18687 (78)
I Live In Turkey
I'm A Vamp From East Broadway

45

Sung by Fannie Brice
The Leg of Nation's
The Syncopated Vamp
Tell Me, Little Gypsy
Sung by John Steel
John Steel, Victor 18687 (78)

Tell Me, Little Gypsy (a) Art Hickman's Orch-
Bells   (b) estra, Columbia A2972
                             (78)

1921:

All By Myself
  Al Jolson, Decca DL-9099 (33-1/3)
  Al Jolson and Bing Crosby (medley), V-Disc 814
  (12") (78)
  Don Cherry (with Grady Martin and Slew Foot
  Five), Decca 28635 (78)
  Frank Crumit, Columbia A3415 (78)
  Bobby Darin, Capitol T-1791 (33-1/3); Scripto,
  Inc., premium record (45) (ep)
  Frankie Froeba (piano), Decca 27826; Decca DL-
  5372 (33-1/3)
  Glen Gray and Casa Loma Orchestra, Coral 60324
  (78)
  Benny Krueger's Orchestra, Brunswick 2130 (78)
  Ted Lewis Jazz Band, Columbia A3434 (78)
  McGuire Sisters, Coral CRL-57026 (33-1/3)
At The Court Around The Corner
The Passion Flower
Pickanniny Mose
There's A Corner Up In Heaven
I Like It
  (also known as "I'm Gonna Do It If I Like It
  (And I Like It)")

Featured in show "Ziegfeld's 9 O'Clock Frolic".
Arthur Hall, Cleartone C-55 (78)
Marion Harris, Columbia A3367 (78)

On September 22, 1921, Irving Berlin and Sam H.
Harris opened their new Music Box Theatre with
the presentation of their first annual "The Music
Box Revue". Berlin wrote every song himself, and
appeared in the cast along with Ethylind Terry,
Willie Collier, Florence Moore, Sam Bernard, Ivy
Sawyer, Joseph Santley, Emma Haig, Paul Frawley,
Brox Sisters and Wilda Bennett. Berlin score:

Behind The Fan
Dancing The Seasons Away
  Sung and danced by Sam Bernard and Rene Riano.
Everybody Step
  Sung by Brox Sisters.
  Ted Lewis Jazz Band, Columbia A3499 (78)
I'm A Dumb-Bell
  Sung by Rene Riano.
In A Cozy Kitchenette Apartment
The Legend Of The Pearls
  Sung by Wilda Bennett.
My Ben Ali Haggin Girl
My Little Book Of Poetry
Say It With Music
  First sung by Wilda Bennett and Paul Frawley;
  later by Ethylind Terry and Joseph Santley.
  This was to have served as the title of a 1939
  20th Century Fox filmusical, score entirely
  comprised of old and new Berlin tunes, which
  somehow was never filmed.
  John Steel, Victor 18828 (78)
  Fred Waring Glee Club, Decca 29063 (78); Decca
  DL-8082 (33-1/3)

Paul Whiteman Orchestra, Victor 18803 (78)
The Schoolhouse Blues
They Call It Dancing
  Sung by Sam Bernard.
  Al Herman, Columbia A3507 (78)
  Georgie Jessel, Cabot CAB-1001 (33-1/3)

The Call It Dancing   (a) Paul Whiteman Orchestra,
The Schoolhouse   (b) Victor 18856 (78)
  Blues

1922:

Funny Feet
Homesick
  Nora Bayes, Columbia A3711 (78)
  Arthur Fields, Cameo 277 (78)
  Ted Lewis Jazz Band (whistling by Ted Lewis),
  Columbia A3709 (78)
  Billy Murray and Ed Smalle, Victor 18982 (78)
The Little Red Lacquer Cage
Mont Marte
Rainy Day Sue
Some Sunny Day
  Eddie Condon Orchestra, Decca 23721 [Album A-
  490] (78); Decca DL-5218 (33-1/3)
  Bing Crosby, RCA Victor LPM-1473 (33-1/3)
  Marion Harris, Columbia A3593 (78)
  Irving Kaufman, Vocalion 14344 (78)

On October 23, 1922, Berlin and Harris presented
their second "The Music Box Revue". In the cast
were Bobby Clark and Paul McCullough, Charlotte
Greenwood, Grace LaRue, William Gaxton, John
Steel, the Fairbanks Twins, and the McCarthy
Sisters. Berlin score:

Bring On The Pepper
Sung by McCarthy Sisters. The chorus contains
a reference to George M. Cohan.
Brox Sisters (with Bennie Krueger's Orchestra),
Brunswick 2360 (78)
Crinoline Days
Sung by Grace LaRue.
Hugh Donovan, Banner 1160 (78)
Paul Whiteman Orchestra, Victor 18983 (78)
Dance Your Troubles Away
I'm Looking For A Daddy Long Legs
Sung by Charlotte Greenwood
Lady Of The Evening
Sung by John Steel
Fred Astaire, Kapp KL-1165 (33-1/3)
Billy Daniels, Mercury EP-1-3035 (45) (ep)
John Steel, Victor 18990 (78)
My Diamond Horseshoe Of Girls
Interpolating an operatic parody wherein six
famous opera characters were played and bur-
lesqued by Grace LaRue, Bobby Clark, William
Gaxton, and three other stars.
Pack Up Your Sins (And Go To The Devil)
Sung by McCarthy Sisters.
Emil Coleman and his Montmarte Orchestra,
Vocalion 14462 (78)
Paul Whiteman Orchestra, Victor 18983 (78)
Porcelain Maid
Emil Coleman and his Montmarte Orchestra,
Vocalion 14462 (78)
Take A Little Wife
Three·Cheers For The Red, White, And Blue
Too Many Girls
Will She Come From The East (North, West, Or South)?
Sung by John Steel.
John Steel, Victor 18990 (78)

His Royal Shyness
    An unpublished number written to flatter the
    Prince Of Wales on his visit to America.
If You Know How To Strut
Tell All The Folks In Kentucky (I'm Comin' Home)
Tell Me With A Melody
Um-Um-Da-Da

On September 22, 1923, Berlin and Harris presented
their third "The Music Box Revue". The cast in-
cluded Robert Benchley, Grace Moore, Florence
Moore, Joseph Santley, Mademoiselle Dora Stroeva,
Frank Tinney, Lora Sonderson, John Steel, Ivy
Sawyer, Solly Ward, Florence O'Denishawn, Phil
Baker, Hugh Cameron, and the Brox Sisters. Berlin
score:

An Orange Grove In California
    Sung by Grace Moore and John Steel.
    John Steel, Victor 19219 (78)
Climbing Up The Scale
Learn To Do The Strut
    Sung by Brox Sisters
    Brox Sisters, Brunswick 2538 (78)
Little Butterfly
    John Steel, Victor 19219 (78)
Maid Of Mesh
    Sung by Ivy Sawyer and Joseph Santley.
One Girl
Tell Me A Bedtime Story
Too Many Sweethearts
The Waltz Of Long Ago
    Sung by Grace Moore.

When You Walked Out Someone Else Walked Right In
  Frank Crumit, Columbia A3933 (78)
  Brooke Johns Orchestra (with vocal chorus), Victor 19092 (78)
Your Hat And My Hat
Yes! We Have No Bananas
  The original of this terrible song was written
  by Frank Silver and Irving Cohn, of course, but
  Irving Berlin enlarged it into an operatic
  parody on those arias given below. This arrange-
  ment was performed in "The Music Box Revue" by
  Florence Moore, Frank Tinney, Lora Sonderson,
  Joseph Santley, Grace Moore and John Steel. It
  was again sung by Al Jolson (with Minstrel
  Ensemble) in his 1930 film "Mammy", at which
  time Berlin adapted it so that the Jolson part
  would dominate. These were by-and-large the
  same operatic segments as burlesqued in Berlin's
  "Diamond Horseshoe" number the year before.

  (a) "Triumphal March" from "Aida"
  (b) "Chi Mi Frena?" from "Lucia Di Lammermoor"
  (c) "Bella Figlia Dell' Amore" from "Rigoletto"
  (d) "Belle Nuit (O, Nuit D'Amore)" from "Contes
      D'Hoffmann"
  (e) "Ah! Che La Morte Ognora" from "Il Trovatore"
  (f) "Anvil Chorus" from "Il Trovatore"
  (g) "Hallelujah Chorus" from "The Messiah"

                    1924:

Lazy
  Popularized and probably introduced by Al Jolson.
  Al Jolson (1924), Brunswick 2595 (78)
  Al Jolson (1947), V-Disc 780 (12") (78)
  Brox Sisters, Victor 19298 (78)

                    51

California Ramblers (orchestra), Columbia
105-D (78)
Vaughn DeLeath, Gennett 5425 (78)
Mitzi Gaynor, Verve MGV-2110 (33-1/3)
Dolores Gray, Decca 90059 (12") (78)
Ernest Hare, Regal 9636 (78)
Irving Kaufman, Vocalion 14791 (78)
Beatrice Lillie (medley), London 5471 (33-1/3)
Marilyn Monroe, 20th Fox FXG-5000 (33-1/3)
Blossom Seeley, Columbia 114-D (78); Columbia
CL-2230 [Album C3L-35] (33-1/3)
Paul Whiteman Orchestra, Victor 19299 (78)
We'll All Go Voting For Al
    (melody based on Blake and Lawlor's "The Side-
    walks Of New York")
    Campaign song for successful New York Guber-
    natorial Candidate Alfred E. Smith.
What'll I Do
    This was the first of Berlin's great love-
    ballads written during his beleaguered
    courtship of Ellen Mackay. It proved such a
    hit - including being sung over the radio by
    operatic singer Frances Alda in a special
    broadcast honoring Berlin - that he interpolate
    it into the score of his third "Music Box Revue
    (still running from the previous year) wherein
    it was sung with further success by Grace Moore
    Al Jolson, Decca DL-9070 (33-1/3)
    Frances Alda, Victrola 1032 (78)
    Norman Brooks, Promenade 2107/Golden Tone
    C4048 (33-1/3)
    Henry Burr and Marcia Freer, Victor 19301 (78)
    Georgia Gibbs, Mercury MG-25199 (33-1/3)
    Dick Haymes, Decca 27446 (78); Decca DL-5291
    (33-1/3)
    Judy Holliday, Columbia CL-1153 (33-1/3)

Irving Kaufman, Vocalion 14797 (78)
Wayne King Orchestra, V-Disc 725 (12") (78)
Gisele MacKenzie, Capitol 2059 (78)
Dinah Shore, RCA Victor 45-0008 (78)
Frank Sinatra (1947), Columbia 38045 (78)
Frank Sinatra (1962), Reprise F-1007 (33-1/3)
Frank Sterling and Charles Warren, Perfect
12116 (78)
Victor Salon Orchestra, Victor 19876 (78)
All Alone
The second of Berlin's great love-ballads
written for Ellen. This also was such a hit -
including being sung on the same radio broad-
cast by operatic singer John McCormack - that
Berlin interpolated it into the score of his
upcoming fourth "Music Box Revue" (see below)
wherein it was featured by Grace Moore and
Oscar Shaw, singing to each other into lighted
telephones at opposite ends of the stage.
Al Jolson (1924), Brunswick 2743 (78)
Al Jolson (1947) (piano, Oscar Levant), Decca
DL-9095 (33-1/3)
Connee Boswell, Decca 1889 (78)
Bing Crosby, Longine Symphonette Society LWS-
224 (33-1/3)
Georgia Gibbs, Mercury MG-25199 (33-1/3)
Lewis James, Victor 19495 (78)
The Jesters (medley), Decca 24358 (78)
Wayne King Orchestra, V-Disc 725 (12") (78)
John McCormack, Victrola 1067(78)
Dinah Shore, Bluebird B-11278 (78)
Frank Sinatra, Reprise F-1007 (33-1/3)
Victor Salon Orchestra, Victor 20321 (78)

On December 1, 1924, Berlin and Harris presented
their fourth and final "The Music Box Revue".

53

Grace Moore (overjoyed that John Steel was no longer in the show) appeared with the Brox Sisters (a last-minute replacement for the Duncan Sisters), Fannie Brice, Bobby Clark and Paul McCullough, Tamara and Margarita, Oscar Shaw, Ula Sharon, Carl Randall, and Claire Booth Luce. Berlin score:

Bandana Ball
The Call Of The South
    Sung by Grace Moore as a counter-melody to
    Stephen Foster's "Old Folks At Home".
    The verse contains a reference to Al Jolson,
    who revived this number in his 1930 film
    "Mammy". For recordings, consult same.
Come Along With Alice
    Sung by Brox Sisters; danced by Ula Sharon
    and Carl Randall.
A Couple Of Senseless Censors
Don't Send Me Back To Petrograd
    Sung by Fannie Brice
The Happy New Year Blues
    Sung on TV, January 11, 1954, by Georgie Jessel
I Want To Be A Ballet Dancer
    Sung and danced by Fannie Brice and Bobby Clark
In The Shade Of A Sheltering Tree
Listening
    Grace Moore, Victor 19613 (78)
Rock-A-Bye Baby
    Sung by Grace Moore.
    Grace Moore, Victor 19688 (78)
Sixteen, Sweet Sixteen
Tell Her In The Springtime
    Grace Moore, Victor 19613 (78)
Tokyo Blues

Sung by Brox Sisters; danced by Tamara and Margarita.
Unlucky In Love
Where Is My Little Old New York?
Who
Wildcats
Danced by Claire Booth Luce.

1925:

Remember
(original and correct title: "You Forgot To Remember")
The third great love-ballad Irving Berlin wrote for Ellen Mackay. Sung by Kathryn Grayson (as Grace Moore) in 1953 film "The Grace Moore Story".
Al Jolson (1925), Brunswick 3013 (78)
Al Jolson (1948), Decca 30600 (78); Decca DL-9099 (33-1/3)
Kenny Baker, Victor 26664 (78)
Connee Boswell, Decca 1889 (78)
Henry Burr (saxophone, Rudy Wiedoeft), Victor 19780 (78)
Jesse Crawford (organ), Victor 19906 (78)
Erskine Hawkins Orchestra, RCA Victor 20-1639 (78)
Tony Martin, RCA Victor 20-3573 (78); RCA Victor 45-3069 (45)
John McCormack, Victrola 1121 (78)
Dinah Shore, V-Disc 643 (12") (78)
Dinah Shore, RCA Victor 45-0009 (78)
Frank Sinatra, Reprise F-1007 (33-1/3)
Always
This love-ballad was Berlin's wedding present to Ellen - not the sentiment alone, but also all ownership rights and royalties, which by 1946

came to $60,000. Sung by Deanna Durbin (to
Gene Kelly) in 1944 film "Christmas Holiday".
Al Jolson, Decca DL-9050 (33-1/3)
Henry Burr, Victor 19959 (78)
Jeff Chandler, Decca 29345 (78)
Jesse Crawford (organ), Victor 20000 (78)
Bing Crosby ("blow-up"), Dick Haymes, Dennis
Day, Andy Russell, V-Disc 773 (12") (78)
Deanna Durbin, Decca 23397 (78)
Joan Edwards, V-Disc 108/V-Disc 328 (12")
(78)
Eileen Farrell, Decca 24140 (78)
Kathryn Grayson, MGM 30283 (78); Lion L70055
(33-1/3)
Ink Spots, Decca 24140 (78)
Gordon Jenkins Orchestra, Capitol 125 (78)
Irving Kaufman, Perfect 12243 (78)
Kay Kyser Orchestra (medley), V-Disc 236 (12")
(78)
Guy Lombardo and his Royal Canadians, Decca
23817 (78)
Grace Moore, RCA Victor 10-1171 (78); RCA
Camden CAL-519 (33-1/3)
Dinah Shore, RCA Victor 45-0010 (78)
Frank Sinatra (1947), Columbia CL-1359 (33-1/3)
Frank Sinatra (1960), Capitol W-1491 (33-1/3)
Ann Southern, Tops L1611 (33-1/3)
Victor Salon Orchestra, Victor 19972 (78)
Don't Wait Too Long
He Doesn't Know What It's All About
It's A Walk-In With Walker
  Campaign song for successful New York Mayoral
  Candidate James J. Walker.
Tango Melody
They're Blaming The Charleston
Venetian Isles

Berlin's next Broadway show was "The Cocoanuts".
The Marx Brothers (Groucho, Harpo, Chico, Zeppo)
headed a cast that included Frances Williams,
Janet Velie, Margaret Dumont, Jerry Whyte, and
the Brox Sisters. Berlin score:

Everyone In The World (Is Doing The Charleston)
Family Reputation
Five O'Clock Tea
Florida By The Sea
Gentlemen Prefer Blondes
    (title taken from that novel by Anita Loos)
A Little Bungalow
    Franklin Baur and Helen Clark, Victor 19974 (78)
Lucky Boy
Minstrel Days
Monkey Doodle Doo
    Sung by Brox Sisters. Was this the same "Monkey
    Doodle Doo" written by Berlin in 1913, or did
    he use this title twice?
The Tale Of A Shirt
Ting-A-Ling (The Bells'll Ring)
    Jesse Crawford (organ), Victor 20263 (78)
    Fred Rich and his Hotel Astor Orchestra (vocal
    by Ray Stillwell), Columbia 720-D (78)
Too Many Sweethearts
    Was this the same "Too Many Sweethearts" written
    by Berlin in 1923 for the third "Music Box
    Revue", or did he use the title twice?
We Should Care
Why Am I A Hit With The Ladies?

A Medley of "Gems From 'The Cocoanuts'" was
recorded by Victor Light Opera Company as Part 1/
Part 2 of Victor 35769 (12") (78).

1926:

At Peace With The World
  Another song for Ellen, this one reflecting the
  contentment of happy married life.
  Sung by Georgie Jessel in Vitaphone one-reel
  short subject.
  Al Jolson, Brunswick 3196 (78)
  Jesse Crawford (organ), Victor 20075 (78)
Because I Love You
  Introduced by Al Jolson.
  Henry Burr, Victor 20258 (78)
  John McCormack, Victrola 1215 (78)
  Victor Orchestra (conducted by Nat Shilkret),
  Victor 20272 (78)
  Victor Salon Orchestra, Victor 20433 (78)
How Many Times?
  (title sometimes incorrectly given as "How Many
  Times Must I Tell You I Love You?")
  Featured in 1929 film "The Time, The Place, And
  The Girl".
  Brox Sisters, Victor 20123 (78)
  Buffalodians (with vocal chorus), Regal 8088 (78)
  Bobby Byrne (trombone solo) and his Orchestra,
  Decca 3942 (78)
  Happiness Boys (Billy Jones and Ernest Hare),
  Columbia 700-D (78)
  Irving Kaufman, Harmony 205-H/Velvet Tone 1205-
  V/Diva 2205-G (78)
  Seattle Harmony Kings, Victor 20133 (78)
  Orrin Tucker (vocal) and his Orchestra, Col-
  umbia 35228 (78)
I'm On My Way Home
  Whispering Jack Smith, Victor 20229 (78)
Just A Little Longer
  Honey Duke and His Uke (Johnny Marvin),
  Harmony 284-H/Velvet Tone 1284-V/Diva 2284-G
  (78)

Peerless Quartette, Victor 20335 (78)
Phil Spitalny's Orchestra (vocal by Charles Hart)
Victor 20272 (78)
My Baby's Come Back To Me
That's A Good Girl
  Roger Wolfe Kahn Orchestra, Victor 20243 (78)
  Whispering Jack Smith, Victor 20254 (78)
Why Do You Want To Know Why?
  Ipana Troubadours (vocal by·Franklin Baur),
  Columbia 696-D (78)
Blue Skies
  Although this was one of the big 1927 hits, it
  was actually introduced on December 28, 1926,
  in the Rodgers & Hart show "Betsy", by Irving
  Berlin's favorite female vocalist, for whom he
  wrote it, Belle Baker. It was sung by Berlin's
  favorite male vocalist, Al Jolson, in 1927
  film "The Jazz Singer", and Al recorded it for
  his 1946 bio-pic "The Jolson Story", in which
  it wasn't used. Sung, probably by Eddie Cantor,
  in 1929 film "Glorifying The American Girl".
  Charlie Barnet Orchestra, V-Disc 458/V-Disc 864
  (12") (78)
  Norman Brooks, Promenade 2107/Piourette FM-3/
  Coronet CX-45 (33-1/3)
  Carol Bruce, Tops L1574 (33-1/3)
  Robinson Cleaver (pipe organ), Decca 27959
  (78)
  Perry Como (with Satisfiers), RCA Victor
  20-1917 (78)
  Jesse Crawford (organ), Victor 20459 (78)
  Vaughn DeLeath, Edison 51948 (78)
  Vaughn DeLeath, Okeh 40750/French Odeon 165089
  (78)
  Jimmy Dorsey Orchestra, Decca 18385 (78)
  Tommy Dorsey Orchestra, V-Disc 1 (12") (78)

Tommy Dorsey Orchestra (vocal by Frank Sinatra),
RCA Victor LPM-1433 (33-1/3)
Ella Fitzgerald (with Buddy Rich), V-Disc 775
(12") (78)
Benny Goodman Orchestra, Columbia 37053 (78)
Jerry Gray Orchestra, Decca 24980 (78)
Woody Herman Orchestra, V-Disc 458 (12") (78)
Betty Hutton, Capitol 188 (78)
Fritz Kreisler (violin), Victrola 1233 (78)
Ted Lewis (vocal) and his Orchestra, Decca
24968 (78); Decca DL-5233 (33-1/3)
Beatrice Lillie (medley), London 5212 (33-1/3)
Johnny Long Orchestra (vocal by Bob Houston
and Ensemble), Decca 23622 (78)
Johnny Marvin and Ed Smalle, Victor 20457 (78)
McGuire Sisters, Coral CRL-57026 (33-1/3)
Glenn Miller Orchestra, Bluebird B10087 (78)
Les Paul Trio, Decca 23553/Decca 27903 (78)
Harry Richman, Vocalion 15511 (78)
Dinah Shore, RCA Victor 45-0007 (78)
Frank Sinatra, Columbia CL-902 (33-1/3)

1927:

In Those Good Old Bowery Days
Russian Lullaby
Bunny Berigan Orchestra (vocal by Kathleen
Lane), RCA Victor 20-1501 (78)
Jesse Crawford (organ), Victor 20791 (78)
Guy Lombardo and his Royal Canadians (vocal
by Jimmy Brown   Decca 23762/24040 (78)
Dinah Shore, RCA Victor 45-0010 (78)
Noel Taylor (Irving Kaufman), Okeh 40808 (78)
Victor Salon Orchestra, Victor 20733 (78)
Teddy Wilson (piano), V-Disc 16 (12") (78)
The Song Is Ended (But The Melody Lingers On)

Louis Armstrong and Mills Brothers, Decca 1892
(78); Decca DL-5509 (33-1/3)
Joe Bishop Orchestra, V-Disc 874 (12") (78)
Jesse Crawford (organ), Victor 21092 (78)
Ruth Etting, Columbia 1196-D (78)
Nellie Lutcher, Capitol 40063 (78)
Frank Sinatra, Reprise F-1007 (33-1/3)
Reinald Werrenrath, Victrola 1310 (78)
Together, We Two
Vaughn DeLeath and Ed Smalle, Victor 21042 (78)
Ruth Etting, Columbia 1196-D (78)
What Does It Matter?
Sung over NBC radio from Memphis, Tennessee,
April 30, 1927, by Al Jolson.
Henry Burr, Victor 20490 (78)
Jesse Crawford (organ), Victor 20560 (78)
Harry Richman, Brunswick 3501 (78)
What Makes Me Love You
Why I Love My Baby
Why Should He Fly At So Much A Week (When He
Could Be The Shiek Of Paree)?
Another dreary topical song about Charles A.
Lindbergh's flight across the Atlantic.

Irving Berlin became the only composer to write
an entire Ziegfeld Follies score in fashioning
that for the "Ziegfeld Follies of 1927". Eddie
Cantor, star and thereby the only entertainer to
attain sole stardom in a Follies, was supported
by Ruth Etting, Franklin Baur, Harry McNaughton,
Dan Healy, Andrew Tombes, Lora Foster, Frances
Upton, The Twin Pianos, Irene Delroy, Claire
Boothe Luce, and the Brox Sisters. Berlin score:

I Want To Be Glorified
It All Belongs To Me

Sung by Eddie Cantor.
  Ruth Etting, Columbia 1113-D (78)
It's Up To The Band
  Sung by Brox Sisters.
Jimmy
Jungle Jingle
  Danced by Claire Booth Luce.
Learn To Sing A Love Song
  Sung by Eddie Cantor.
My New York
Ooh! Maybe It's You
Rainbow Of Girls
  Sung by Franklin Baur.
Ribbons And Bows
Shaking The Blues Away
  Sung by Ruth Etting. Reprised by Doris Day (as
  Miss Etting) in 1955 bio-pic "Love Me Or Leave
  Me".
  Doris Day, Columbia CL-710 (33-1/3)
  Ruth Etting, Columbia1113-D (78); Columbia ML-
  5050 (33-1/3)
  Lisa Kirk, Sinclair OSS-2250 (33-1/3)
Tickling The Ivories
You Gotta Have IT
  Sung by Eddie Cantor. This was Irving Berlin's
  rewrite of a song written by Cantor during 1926,
  "I'm So Broken Hearted 'Cause I Haven't Got IT".

The following Medley was truly an "original cast"
recording, with the vocals of Franklin Baur and
the Brox Sisters, and the twin pianos of Fairchild
& Rainger. Baur's chorus of "Rainbow Of Girls"
was reissued on the 12" LP RCA Victor LOC-1011
(33-1/3).

ZIEGFELD FOLLIES MEDLEY,
Nat Shilkret and the Victor Orchestra,
Victor 35845 (12") (78)

Part 1

Shaking The Blues Away (FAIRCHILD and RAINGER)
Ooh! Maybe It's You (BROX SISTERS)
Jungle Jingle (FAIRCHILD and RAINGER)
Rainbow Of Girls (FRANKLIN BAUR)
Shaking The Blues Away (FAIRCHILD and RAINGER)

Part 2

It All Belongs To Me (BROX SISTERS and FRANKLIN
   BAUR)
Tickling The Ivories (FAIRCHILD and RAINGER)
Ooh! Maybe It's You (FRANKLIN BAUR)
It's Up To The Band (BROX SISTERS)
It All Belongs To Me (FAIRCHILD and RAINGER)

1928:

Evangeline
   (melody by Al Jolson)
   This Jolson-Berlin collaboration was never pub-
   lished, although the following year, Irving
   Berlin, Inc., published a new melody by Al
   Jolson, a new lyric by Billy Rose, to a new
   "Evangeline" which served as Theme-Song for
   the film of that name.
Good Times With Hoover, Better Times With Al
   Campaign song for unsuccessful Presidential
   Candidate Alfred E. Smith.
How About Me?

Jesse Crawford (organ), Victor 21850 (78)
Morton Downey, Victor 21806 (78)
Judy Garland, Capitol T-835 (33-1/3)
Judy Holliday, Columbia CL-1153 (33-1/3)
Fred Waring's Pennsylvanians, Victor 21792 (78)
I Can't Do Without You
  Gene Austin, Victor 21454 (78)
  Jesse Crawford (organ), Victor 21502 (78)
  James Melton, Columbia 1329-D (78)
Roses Of Yesterday
  Jesse Crawford (organ), Victor 21713 (78)
  Lewis James, Victor 21700 (78)
  Fred Waring's Pennsylvanians, Victor 21676 (78)
Sunshine
  Paul Whiteman Orchestra (vocal by Bing Crosby),
  Victor 21240 (78)
To Be Forgotten
  Wayne King Orchestra (vocal by Aragon Trio),
  Victor 22236 (78)
Yascha Michaeloffsky's Melody

following numbers placed as Theme-Songs
in early talking pictures

Marie
  Theme-Song of Vilma Banky film "The Awakening".
  Revived in films "The Fabulous Dorseys" (1947)
  and "Lover Come Back" (1946).
  Louis Armstrong and Mills Brothers, Decca 28984
  (78); Decca DL-5509 (33-1/3)
  Franklin Baur, Victor 21787 (78)
  Broadway Broadcasters (with vocal chorus), Cameo
  8365 (78)
  Tommy Dorsey Orchestra (vocal by Jack Leonard
  and Ensemble), Victor 25523 (78) *

Tommy Dorsey Orchestra (vocal by Frank Sinatra),
Victor 27519 (78); RCA Victor LPM-6003 (33-1/3)
Tommy Dorsey Orchestra, V-Disc 273 (12") (78)
Four Tunes, Jubilee [catalogue number unknown]
(45) *
Frankie Laine, Columbia B-12771 (45) (ep)
The Troubadours, Victor 21746 (78)
Coquette
Theme-Song of Mary Pickford film "Coquette".
Louis Armstrong and Mills Brothers, Decca 4327
(78); Decca DL-5509 (33-1/3)
John Kirby Orchestra, Columbia 35999 [Album C-45]
(78)
Paul Oliver (Frank Munn), Victor 21898 (78)
Rudy Vallee (vocal) and his Connecticut Yankees,
Victor 21880 (78)
Paul Whiteman Orchestra (vocal by Bing Crosby),
Columbia 1755-D (78)
Where Is The Song Of Songs For Me?
Theme-Song of Lupe Velez film "Lady Of The
Pavements"; sung three times therein by Miss
Velez.
Franklin Baur, Victor 21904 (78)
Johnny Hamp's Kentucky Serenaders (vocal by
Joe Cassidy), Victor 21838 (78)
Lupe Velez, Victor 21932 (78)

1929:

I'm The Head Man

following two numbers featured in
Marx Brothers film "The Cocoanuts":

I Lost My Shirt
Unpublished; probably left on cutting-room floor.

When My Dreams Come True
Sung by Mary Eaton and Oscar Shaw.
Franklin Baur, Victor 21989 (78)
Ford and Glenn, Columbia A1841-D (78)
Fred Waring's Pennsylvanians, Victor 21977 (78)
Paul Whiteman Orchestra (with vocal chorus),
Columbia 1822-D (78)

<u>following two numbers featured</u>
<u>in all-Negro film "Hallelujah"</u>:

Swanee Shuffle
Sung by Nina Mae McKinney.
Waiting At The End Of The Road
Sung by Daniel L. Haynes.
All Star Orchestra, Victor 22073 (78)
Daniel L. Haynes (with Dixie Singers), Victor
22097 (78)
Frankie Laine, Mercury 5332 (78)
The Revelers, Victor 22270 (78)
Kay Starr, Capitol H-363 (33-1/3)

<u>following three numbers featured in</u>
<u>Harry Richman film "Puttin' On The Ritz"</u>:

Alice In Wonderland
Technicolor production number in an otherwise
black-and-white film. Rather than being the
same "Alice In Wonderland" written by Berlin
for 1916 show "The Century Girl" (see page 34),
this was actually the number presented as "Come
Along With Alice" in Berlin's 1924 "Music Box
Revue" (see page 54).
Debroy Somers Band (vocal by Trio), British
Columbia CB46 (78)

Puttin' On The Ritz
   Theme-Song of film; sung therein by Harry Rich-
   man to become his personal Theme-Song.
   Fred Astaire (1932), British Columbia DB2270
   (78)
   Fred Astaire (medley) (1959), Kapp KL-1165
   (33-1/3)
   Jan Garber Orchestra (with vocal chorus),
   British Columbia CB46 (78)
   Judy Garland (1960), Capitol T-1467 (33-1/3)
   Judy Garland (April 23, 1961), Capitol WBO-
   1569 (33-1/3)
   Harry Richman (1929), Brunswick 4677 (78)
   Harry Richman (1947), Decca 24391 [Album A-632]
   (78)
With You
   Sung by Harry Richman and Joan Bennett.
   Jack Miller, Publix 2018-P (78)
   Harry Richman, Brunswick 4678 (78)

In addition to the above Irving Berlin score,
Harry Richman also introduced "Singing a Vagabond
Song" (Harry Richman-Val Burton-Sam Messenheimer)
and "There's Danger In Your Eyes, Cherie!" (Harry
Richman-Jack Meskill-Pete Wendling), the latter
written for Clara Bow.

                1929 (songs written):
                1930 (film released):

Al Jolson's film "Mammy" opened at the Warner
Theatre, N.Y., March 26, 1930. In addition to
the Irving Berlin score of six newly introduced
numbers and two revivals, Al reprised "Who Paid
The Rent For Mrs. Rip Van Winkle?" (Afred Bryan-
Fred Fisher), "Why Do They All Take The Night

Boat To Albany?" (Sam M. Lewis-Joe Young-Jean
Schwartz), and sang snatches of others. Filmed
in both black-and-white and Technicolor. Berlin
score:

Here We Are
    Sung by Minstrel Chorus. Unpublished
In The Morning
    Sung by Minstrel Chorus. Published independ-
    ently the preceding year.
The Call Of The South
    Sung by Al Jolson as a counter-melody to
    Stephen Foster's "Old Folks At Home".
    Bing and Gary Crosby, Decca 29147 (78)
    Charles Forsythe and James Kelly, Gennett 6266
    (78)
    Paul Whiteman Orchestra, Victor 19557 (78)
Knights Of The Road
    Sung by Al Jolson (with Hobo Chorus). Un-
    published.
Let Me Sing - And I'm Happy
    Theme-Song of film; sung three times therein
    by Al Jolson. Also sung by Jolson in 1946 film
    "The Jolson Story"; film-clip used in "Jolson
    Sings Again" (1949).
    Al Jolson (1930), Brunswick 4721 (78); Ace of
    Hearts AH-33 (33-1/3)
    Al Jolson (1947), Decca 24296 (78); Decca DL-
    5031 (10")/DL-9036 (12") (33-1/3)
    Gene Austin, Victor 22341 (78)
    Keefe Braselle, Coral CRL-57295 (33-1/3)
    Norman Brooks, Promenade 2238/Parade SP-351/
    Spinorama MK-3051 (33-1/3)
    Doug Elliott, Crown CLP-5040 (33-1/3)
    Ruth Etting, Columbia 2172-D (78)

Sid Garry, Harmony 1130-H/Velvet Tone 2130-V/
Diva 3130-G (78)
Jerry Lewis, Decca 30263 (78); Decca 9-31400
(45)
Frankie Vaughan, Phillips PHM200-006 (33-1/3)
Fred Waring's Pennsylvanians, Victor 22340 (78)
(Across The Breakfast Table) Looking At You
Sung by Al Jolson.
Al Jolson, Brunswick 4721 (78)
Phil Spitalny's Hit-Of-The-Week Orchestra (vocal
by Bill Cody), Hit-Of-The-Week 1071 (78)
Fred Waring's Pennsylvanians, Victor 22340 (78)
To My Mammy
Sung by Al Jolson. Melody of verse retarded
but otherwise the same as verse of Berlin's 1926
"Just A Little Longer".
Al Jolson, Brunswick 4722 (78)
Gene Austin, Victor 22341 (78)
Sid Garry, Harmony 1130-H/Velvet Tone 2130-V/
Diva 3130-G (78)
Yes! We Have No Bananas [Operatic Parody]
Sung by Al Jolson (with Minstrel Ensemble).

During 1953, British Brunswick reissued Al Jolson's
1930 recordings of selections from this score, on
the following 45 rpm extended-play disc - thus
honoring Jolson and Berlin with release of the
earliest-recorded original cast album in recording history:

AL JOLSON MEMORIAL
British Brunswick OE-9159

Side 1:
Let Me Sing And I'm Happy
To My Mammy

69

Looking At You
When The Little Red Roses Get The Blues
For You (Al Dubin-Joe Burke)*

*not from "Mammy"

1930:

Brokers' Ensemble
Do You Believe Your Eyes - Or Do You Believe Your
  Baby?
How Much I Love You
If You Believe
  During 1940, Berlin revised both lyrics and
  melody of this pop/sacred selection. During
  the early 1950's, when Norman Brooks withdrew
  from the Berlin film "There's No Business Like
  Show Business" due to the brevity of his part
  (he later appeared for one minute in "Ocean's
  11" and two minutes in "The Best Things In Life
  Are Free"), the role was given to Johnnie Ray,
  whose big number was this revised version.
  Johnnie Ray (sound-track), Decca 90058 (12")
  (78)
  Johnnie Ray, Columbia 40391 (78)
It's Yours
Just A Little While
  Lee Morse (vocal) and her Blue Grass Boys,
  British Columbia DB355 (78)
  The Troubadours (vocal by Frank Munn), Victor
  22543 (78)
The Little Things In Life
  Featured in 1946 film "Lover Come Back".
  Gus Arnheim Orchestra (vocal by Bing Crosby),
  Victor 22580/Bluebird B-7102 (78)

Chick Bullock, Perfect 12677 (78)
Toast To Prohibition
What A Lucky Break For Me
To A Tango Melody
　Sung by Dolores Del Rio in film "The Bad One".
　Was this the same "Tango Melody" written by
　Berlin in 1925, or did he use this title twice?

1931:

Any Love Today?
Chase All Your Cares (And Go To Sleep, Baby)
　(also known as "Sleep, Baby")
How Can I Change My Luck
I'll Miss You In The Evening
I Want You For Myself
Me!
　Ruth Etting, Perfect 12754/Conqueror 7828/
　British Imperial 2601 (78)
　High Hatters (vocal by Frank Luther), Victor
　22780 (78)
Nudist Colony
Police Of New York
Two Cheers Instead Of Three
(Just) Begging For Love
　Contributed to show "Shoot The Works", a
　depression revue providing work for starving
　performers. Berlin received nothing for this
　number, and it was worth it.
　Guy Lombardo and his Royal Canadians (vocal by
　Carmen Lombardo), Columbia 2500-D (78)

following two numbers featured
in film "Reaching For The Moon":

Reaching For The Moon

Also featured in other 1931 film "Top Speed".
Ruth Etting, Columbia 2377-D (78)
Mills Music Masters (vocal by Sid Garry),
Melotone M-12068 (78)
When The Folks High-Up Do That Mean Low-Down
Sung by Bing Crosby and Bebe Daniels

1932:

Say It Isn't So
A previously unpublished number, actually
written several years earlier.
Al Jolson, Decca DL-9050 (33-1/3)
Norman Brooks, Promenade 2238/Parade SP-351/
Spinorama MK-3051 (33-1/3)
Georgia Gibbs, Mercury 70218 (78)
Coleman Hawkins' 52nd Street All-Stars, RCA
Victor 40-0131 [Album HJ-9] (78)
Roberta Lee, Decca 28541 (78)
Julie London, Liberty LRP-3006 (33-1/3)
How Deep Is The Ocean?   (How High Is The Sky?)
Another previously unpublished number, actually
written several years earlier.
Sung by Frank Sinatra in 1952 film "Meet Danny
Wilson".
Al Jolson, Decca DL-9099 (33-1/3)
Carmen Cavallaro (piano), Decca 24060 (78)
Bing Crosby, Brunswick 6406 (78); Columbia CL-
6027/Harmony HL-7094 (33-1/3)
Georgia Gibbs, V-Disc 407 (12") (78)
Dick Haymes, Decca 18781/Decca 23752 (78)
Guy Lombardo and his Royal Canadians, Decca
27503 (78); Decca DL-5330 (33-1/3)
Ethel Merman (1932), Victor 24146 (78); RCA
Camden CAL-745 (33-1/3)

Ethel Merman (1956), Decca DL-8178 [Album DX-153]
(33-1/3)
Gale Robbins, Vik LX-1128 (33-1/3)
Dinah Shore, RCA Victor 45-0007 (78)
Frank Sinatra (1946), Columbia 37257 [Album C-124] (78)
Frank Sinatra (1960), Capitol W-1417 (33-1/3)
Kate Smith, RCA Victor LPM-2819 (33-1/3)
Kay Starr, RCA Victor LPM-1720 (33-1/3)
Dinah Washington, Mercury 8192 (78); Mercury 5510x45 (45)
Margaret Whiting, Capitol 214/Capitol 874 (78)
I'm Playing With Fire
  Charlie's Orchestra (Nazi propaganda vocal;
  second chorus: different lyrics), Propaganda
  Record No. 0118 (78)
  Bing Crosby, Brunswick 6480/British Columbia
  D.B. 1990 (78)
Prohibition
  Was this the same "Prohibition" written by
  Berlin for the "Ziegfeld Follies Of 1919",
  or did he use this title twice?

Berlin returned to Broadway with the show "Face
The Music". Cast included Mary Boland, J. Harold
Murray, Hugh O'Connell, Andrew Tombes, and
Katherine Carrington. Berlin score:

Dear Old Crinoline Days
I Don't Wanna Be Married (I Just Wanna Be Friends)
I Say It's Spinach - And The Hell With It
  (title taken from caption of cartoon by Carl
  Rose)
Let's Have Another Cup O' Coffee
  Introduced by Katherine Carrington to become
  the hit of the show.

Lunching At The Automat
Manhattan Madness
My Beautiful Rhinestone Girl
On A Roof In Manhattan
Soft Lights And Sweet Music
    Tony Martin, RCA Victor LPM-2107 (33-1/3)
Torch Song
You Must Be Born With It

A Medley of six "Gems From 'Face The Music'" was
recorded by Victor Young and the Brunswick Orchestra on Brunswick 20106 (12") (78). All were
instrumental except for vocal choruses of "Soft
Lights and Sweet Music" (Part 1; Bing Crosby)
and "Let's Have Another Cup O' Coffee" (Part 2;
vocalist unidentified).

1933:

Debts
Eighteenth Amendment Repealed
    (melody based on Stephen Foster's "Old Black
    Joe")
I Can't Remember
    Eddy Duchin Orchestra (vocal by Lew Sherwood),
    Victor 24280 (78)
    Wayne King Orchestra, Columbia 36131 (78)
Maybe I Love You Too Much
    Leo Reisman Orchestra (vocal by Fred Astaire),
    Victor 24262 (78); "X" LVA-1001 (33-1/3)
Metropolitan Opening
Skate With Me
Society Wedding

Irving Berlin set himself the challenge of writing
a song to parallel each feature of a Sunday news-

paper for the show "As Thousands Cheer".
Featured were Marilyn Miller, Ethel Waters,
Clifton Webb, Helen Broderick, Hal Forde, Jose
Limon, Letitia Ide, J. Harold Murray, Hamtree
Harrington, and the Weidman Dancers. Berlin
score:

Easter Parade
  Sung by Marilyn Miller and Clifton Webb with
  Ensemble. Melody of chorus begins the same as
  chorus of Berlin's 1917 "Smile And Show Your
  Dimple".
  Al Jolson, Decca 30600 (78); Decca DL-9063
  (33-1/3)
  Al Jolson and Bing Crosby (medley), V-Disc 814
  (12") (78)
  Norman Brooks, Promenade 2107/Golden Tone C4048
  (33-1/3)
  Perry Como, RCA Victor 20-2142 (78)
  Eddy Duchin (piano), Columbia 35702 [Album C-32]
  (78)
  Harry James Orchestra, Columbia 36545 (78) *
  Harry James Orchestra, V-Disc 138 (12") (78)
  Sammy Kaye Orchestra (vocal by Kaydets),
  Victor 27811/RCA Victor 20-1568 (78)
  Guy Lombardo and his Royal Canadians, Decca
  23817 (78) *
  Leo Reisman Orchestra (vocal by Clifton Webb),
  Victor 24418 (78)
  Andy Russell, Capitol 15034 (78)
  Ethel Smith (console organ), Decca 24321 (78)
  Kate Smith, MGM 10220 (78)
  Fred Waring Glee Club (solo by Gordon Goodman),
  Decca 29063 (78); Decca DL-8082 (33-1/3)
The Funnies
  Sung by Marilyn Miller.

75

Harlem On My Mind
  Sung by Ethel Waters in a take-off on Josephine
  Baker.
  Ethel Waters, Columbia 2826-D (78); Jolly
  Roger 5016 (33-1/3)
Heat Wave
  Sung by Ethel Waters; danced by Letitia Ide,
  Joe Limon, and Weidman Dancers.
  Vivian Blaine, Mercury MG-20234 (33-1/3)
  Bing Crosby, Verve MGV-2020/MGM E4203 (33-1/3)
  Dolores Gray, Decca 29380 (10")/Decca 90059 (12")
  (78)
  Marilyn Monroe, 20th Fox FXG-5000 (33-1/3)
  Ethel Waters, Columbia 2826-D (78); Jolly Roger
  5016 (33-1/3)
  Margaret Whiting (with Crew Chiefs), Capitol
  15209 (78)
How's Chances?
  Leo Reisman Orchestra (vocal by Clifton Webb),
  Victor 24418 (78)
Lonely Heart
  Everett Marshall, Decca 15002 (12") (78)
Not For All The Rice In China
  Sung by Clifton Webb.
  Leo Reisman Orchestra (vocal by Clifton Webb),
  Victor 24428 (78)
Our Wedding Day
Revolt In Cuba
  Sung and danced by Jose Limon and Letitia Ide.
Supper Time
  Sung by Ethel Waters. Of all the songs she
  introduced, this was her favorite.
  Barbra Streisand, Columbia CL-2215 (33-1/3)
  Ethel Waters. Mercury MG-20051 (33-1/3);
  Mercury EP-1-3246 (45) (ep)
To Be Or Not To Be

Sung by Ethel Waters and Hamtree Harrington.
We'll All Be In Heaven When The Dollar Goes To Hell
  Introduced by Helen Broderick.

1934:

Butterfingers
Get Thee Behind Me, Satan
  Resuscitated by Berlin for 1936 film "Follow
  The Fleet". For recordings, consult same.
I Never Had A Chance
  Dean Martin, Capitol 3718 (78)
  Georgie Price, Banner 33107 (78)
Moon Over Napoli
So Help Me
  Paul Hamilton Orchestra (vocal by Chick Bullock),
  Vocalion 2721 (78)
Wild About You
  Resuscitated by Berlin for 1940 show "Louisiana
  Purchase".

1935:

Moonlight Maneuvers
There's A Smile On My Face

following five numbers featured in
Fred Astaire-Ginger Rogers film "Top Hat":

Cheek To Cheek
  (melody based on Frederic Chopin's A-Flat Major
  "Polonaise")
  Sung to Ginger Rogers by Fred Astaire
  Fred Astaire, Brunswick 7486 (78); Epic LN-
  3137 (33-1/3)
  Count Basie Orchestra, RCA Victor 20-3449 (78);

RCA Victor 47-2915 (45)
Boswell Sisters, Decca 574 (78)
Norman Brooks, Promenade 2107/Piourette FM-3/
Coronet CX-45 (33-1/3)
Buddy Cole Trio, Capitol 20135 [Album BD-63]
(78)
Bing Crosby, Verve MGV-2020/MGM E4203/MGM E4240
(33-1/3)
Ziggy Elman Orchestra, MGM 10421 (78)
Hugo Montenegro Orchestra, Time 2044 (33-1/3)
Alvino Rey Orchestra, Capitol 57-644 (78)
Frank Sinatra, Capitol W-1069 (33-1/3)
Isn't This A Lovely Day (To Be Caught In The Rain?)
Sung by Fred Astaire; danced by Fred Astaire and
Ginger Rogers.
Fred Astaire (1935), Brunswick 7487 (78)
Fred Astaire (1959), Kapp KL-1165 (33-1/3)
No Strings (I'm Fancy Free)
Sung and danced by Fred Astaire.
Fred Astaire, Brunswick 7486 (78)
Ramona (vocal) and her Gang, Victor 25138 (78)
The Piccolino
Sung by Ginger Rogers; danced by Fred Astaire
and Ginger Rogers.
Fred Astaire, Brunswick 7488 (78)
Top Hat, White Tie, And Tails
Sung and danced by Fred Astaire (with Chorus
Boys).
Louis Armstrong (vocal) and his Orchestra, MGM
E4240 (33-1/3)
Fred Astaire (1935), Brunswick 7487 (78)
Fred Astaire (medley) (1959), Kapp KL-1165
(33-1/3)
Boswell Sisters, Decca 574 (78)
Norman Brooks, Promenade 2238/Parade SP-351/
Spinorama MK-3051 (33-1/3)

Hugo Montenegro Orchestra, Time 2044 (33-1/3)
Mickey Rooney, RCA Victor LPM-1520 (33-1/3)
John Scott Trotter Orchestra, Warner Bros.
W1333 (33-1/3)

1936:

following seven numbers featured in
Fred Astaire-Ginger Rogers film "Follow The Fleet":

But Where Are You?
  Sung by Harriet Hilliard.
  Jane Froman, Decca 11054 (78); Decca DL-6021
  (33-1/3)
  Ozzie Nelson Orchestra (vocal by Harriet
  Hilliard), Brunswick 7607 (78)
Get Thee Behind Me, Satan
  Sung by Harriet Hilliard.
  Will Bradley Orchestra, Columbia 36248 (78)
  Ozzie Nelson Orchestra (vocal by Harriet
  Hilliard), Brunswick 7607 (78)
I'd Rather Lead A Band
  Sung and danced by Fred Astaire.
  Fred Astaire, Brunswick 7610 (78)
  Larry Foster (parody), Micro 58 (33-1/3)
  Glen Gray and Casa Loma Orchestra (vocal by
  Pee Wee Hunt), Decca 696 (78)
I'm Putting All My Eggs In One Basket
  Sung to Ginger Rogers by Fred Astaire.
  Louis Armstrong (vocal) and his Orchestra,
  Decca 698 (78)
  Fred Astaire, Brunswick 7609 (78)
Let's Face The Music And Dance
  Sung by Fred Astaire; danced by Fred Astaire
  and Ginger Rogers.
  Fred Astaire, Brunswick 7608 (78)

Jane Powell, Verve MGV-2023 (33-1/3)
Frank Sinatra, Reprise F-1001 (33-1/3)
Barbra Streisand (medley), Columbia CL-2478
(33-1/3)
Let Yourself Go
    Sung by Ginger Rogers; danced by Fred Astaire
    and Ginger Rogers.
    Fred Astaire, Brunswick 7608 (78)
    Glen Gray and Casa Loma Orchestra (vocal by
    Pee Wee Hunt), Decca 696 (78)
    Gene Kelly, MGM 30139 [Album MGM-30] (78)
    Ginger Rogers, Ace Of Hearts AH-67 (33-1/3)
We Saw The Sea
    Sung by Fred Astaire (with Sailors' Chorus).
    Fred Astaire (with Male Quartette), Brunswick
    7609 (78)

<u>1937:</u>

Let's Make The Most Of Our Dream
What The Well-Dressed Man Will Wear

<u>following nine numbers featured in film "On The
Avenue" with Dick Powell, Alice Faye, Madeline
Carroll, and Ritz Brothers:</u>

The Girl On The Police Gazette
    Sung by Dick Powell.
    Dick Powell, Decca 1150 (78); Decca DL-8837/
    Ace Of Hearts AH-50 (33-1/3)
He Ain't Got Rhythm
    (as sung in film, interpolating an excerpt from
    Berlin's "Cheek To Cheek")
    Sung by Ritz Brothers.
    Benny Goodman Orchestra (vocal by Jimmy Rushing),
    Victor 25505 (78)

I've Got My Love To Keep Me Warm
   Sung by Dick Powell.
   Hadda Brooks Trio, Modern 649 (78)
   Les Brown and his Band Of Renown, Columbia
   38324 (78) *
   Art Lund, MGM 10348 (78)
   Mills Brothers, Decca 24550 (78)
   Ray Noble Orchestra, RCA Victor 20-3302 (78)
   Dick Powell, Decca DL-8837/Ace Of Hearts AH-50
   (33-1/3)
   Frank Sinatra, Reprise F-1001 (33-1/3)
   The Starlighters, Capitol 15330 (78)
   United States Maritime Service Training Station
   Band, V-Disc 545 (12") (78)
On The Avenue
   Withdrawn from film.
On The Steps Of Grant's Tomb
   Withdrawn from film.
Slumming On Park Avenue
   Sung by Alice Faye.
   Alice Faye, Brunswick 7825 (78)
Swing Sister
   Withdrawn from film.
This Year's Kisses
   Sung by Alice Faye.
   Alice Faye (1937), Brunswick 7825 (78)
   Alice Faye (1961), Reprise R-6029 (33-1/3)
   Benny Goodman Orchestra (vocal by Margaret
   McCrae), Victor 25505 (78)
   Dick Powell, Decca DL-8837/Ace Of Hearts AH-50
   (33-1/3)
You're Laughing At Me
   Sung by Dick Powell. This was Fannie Brice's
   favorite song.
   Dick Powell, Decca 1150 (78)

1938:

Following the premature death of George Gershwin, July 11, 1937, certain of his contemporaries were each asked to contribute an appreciation for inclusion in a eulogistic anthology that was later published. This untitled poem, written May 16, 1938, was Berlin's.

I could speak of a Whiteman rehearsal
At the old Palais Royal when Paul
Played the "Rhapsody" that lifted Gershwin
From the "Alley" to Carnegie Hall.
I could dwell on the talent that placed him
In the class where he justly belongs,
But this verse is a song-writer's tribute
To a man who wrote wonderful songs.

His were tunes that had more than just rhythm,
For just rhythm will soon gather "corn",
And those melodies written by Gershwin
Are as fresh now as when they were born.
As a writer of serious music,
He could dream for a while in the stars,
And step down from the heights of Grand Opera
To a chorus of thirty-two bars.

And this morning's Variety tells me
That the last song he wrote is a hit
It's on top of the list of best sellers,
And the air-waves are ringing with it.
It remains with the dozens of others,
Though the man who composed them is gone;
For a song-writer's job may be ended,
But his melodies linger on.

God Bless America
  A previously unpublished number, actually
  written during 1918 as a Finale for "Yip, Yip,
  Yaphank", but put aside because Berlin feared
  the critics would accuse him of "flag-waving".
  It was first sung publicly by Kate Smith on the
  radio, November 11, 1938, when it created such
  a tsimmis that it came to be termed "America's
  Second National Anthem". All royalties donated
  to Boy and Girl Scouts of America.
  Bing Crosby, Decca 2400/Decca 23579 [Album
  DA-453] (78)
  Deanna Durbin, Decca 18575 (78)
  Horace Heidt and his Musical Knights, Columbia
  35637 (78)
  Jane Pickens, RCA Victor 20-3903 (78)
  Kate Smith (1930's), Victor 26198 (78)
  Kate Smith (1940's), MGM 30025 (78); MGM E4240
  (33-1/3)
  Kate Smith (1950's), Tops L1705 (33-1/3)
  Kate Smith (1960's), RCA Victor LPM-2819 (33-1/3)
  Leopold Stokowski and All-American Orchestra,
  Columbia 17204-D (12") (78)
  12,000 Girl Scouts, United Artists GSEP-2 (33-1/3)
  Fred Waring's Pennsylvanians, Decca 28512 (78)
  Margaret Whiting (with Pied Pipers), Captiol
  15003 (78)
  Barry Wood (with Lehman Engel Singers), Columbia
  35569 (78)
Since They Turned Loch Lomond Into Swing
We'll Never Know
  Another previously unpublished number, actually
  written during 1926.
  Benny Goodman Orchestra (vocal by Martha Tilton),
  Victor 26134 (78)
You Can Be My Cave Man

Care-Free
  Vocal deleted; instrumental background for
  Astaire's golf-stroke dance.
Change Partners
  Sung to Ginger Rogers by Fred Astaire.
  Fred Astaire (1938), Brunswick 8189 (78); Epic
  LN-3137 (33-1/3)
  Fred Astaire (1959), Kapp KL-1165 (33-1/3)
I Used To Be Color Blind
  Sung and danced by Fred Astaire.
  Fred Astaire (1938), Brunswick 8189 (78)
  Fred Astaire (1960), Verve V-2114 (33-1/3)
The Night Is Filled With Music
  Vocal deleted; used as instrumental background.
The Yam
  Sung by Ginger Rogers; danced by Fred Astaire
  and Ginger Rogers.
  Fred Astaire (singing & dancing), Brunswick
  8190 (78)
  Fred Astaire (talking & dancing), Brunswick
  8190 (78)

While there had been filmusicals with new songs
by one composer or old songs by several, the
first with a score comprised of hit oldies by
only one man was Irving Berlin's "Alexander's
Ragtime Band". For this reason, the 20th Century
Fox film starring Tyrone Power, Alice Faye, Don
Ameche, Ethel Merman, Jack Haley, was erroneously
thought by some to be Berlin's life story. His
standards sung therein included the following:
"Alexander's Ragtime Band" (sung twice by Alice
Faye), "All Alone" (Alice Faye), "Blue Skies"

(Alice Faye and Ethel Merman), "Easter Parade"
(Don Ameche), "Everybody's Doing It Now" (Alice
Faye), "Everybody Step" (Ethel Merman), "For
Your Country And My Country" (Army Recruiter),
"Heat Wave" (Ethel Merman), "How Deep Is The Ocean"
(Ethel Merman), "I Can Always Find A Little Sun-
shine In the Y.M.C.A." (Jack Haley), "The Inter-
national Rag" (Alice Faye and Jack Haley), "Oh!
How I Hate To Get Up In The Morning" (Jack Haley),
"Pack Up Your Sins" (Ethel Merman), "A Pretty
Girl Is Like A Melody" (Ethel Merman), "The Rag-
time Violin" (Vocal Trio), "Remember" (Alice
Faye), "Say It With Music" (Ethel Merman), "This
Is The Life" (Wally Vernon), "We're On Our Way
To France" (Soldier Chorus), "When The Midnight
Choo-Choo Leaves For Alabam'" (Alice Faye),
not all of which were sung in full. Instrumental
backgrounds included "Alexander's Ragtime Band",
"Call Me Up Some Rainy Afternoon", "Cheek To
Cheek", In My Harem", "Lazy", "Marie", "Some
Sunny Day", "The Song Is Ended", "What'll I Do",
and "When I Lost You". For this film, Berlin
wrote only the following three new selections
(all of which were recorded by Tony Martin for
Brunswick; catlogue numbers unknown):

I'm Marching Along With Time
My Walking Stick
    Sung by Ethel Merman. Broadcast September 20,
    1938, by Al Jolson.
    Louis Armstrong and Mills Brothers, Decca
    1892/28984 (78); Decca DL-5509 (33-1/3)
Now It Can Be Told
    Sung by Don Ameche; also by Alice Faye.
    Bing Crosby, Decca 1888/Decca 25093 (78)

On August 3, 1938, in conjunction with the release

85

of "Alexander's Ragtime Band", CBS radio pre-
sented a 90-minute salute to Irving Berlin
starring Al Jolson, Ben Bernie, Connee Boswell,
Eddie Cantor, Ted Husing, Bert Lahr, Ethel
Merman, Sophie Tucker, and Berlin himself. On
April 7, 1947, in conjunction with the film's
revival, "The Lux Radio Theatre" broadcast a
radio adaptation starring Al Jolson, Tyrone
Power, Dinah Shore, Dick Haymes, and Margaret
Whiting. Both broadcasts were replete with
Berlin melodies.

1939:

following six numbers featured in film "Second
Fiddle" with Sonja Henie, Tyrone Power, Rudy
Vallee, Edna May Oliver, and Mary Healy:

An Old Fashioned Tune Always Is New
  Jimmy Dorsey Orchestra (vocal by Don Matteson),
  Decca 2553 (78)
  Rudy Vallee, Decca 2552 (78)
Back To Back
  Jimmy Dorsey Orchestra (vocal by Helen O'Con-
  nell), Decca 2554 (78)
  Horace Heidt and Musical Knights (vocal by
  Heidt's High Lights), Brunswick 8393 (78)
I'm Sorry For Myself
  Rudy Vallee, Decca 2552 (78)
I Poured My Heart Into A Song
  Jimmy Dorsey Orchestra (vocal by Bob Eberly),
  Decca 2553 (78)
  Mary Healy, Brunswick 8436 (78)
  Horace Heidt and Musical Knights (vocal by
  Larry Cotton and High Lights), Brunswick 8393(7

86

Artie Shaw Orchestra (vocal by Helen Forrest),
Bluebird B10307 (78)
Rudy Vallee, Decca 2551 (78)
The Song Of The Metronome
Mary Healy, Brunswick 8436 (78)
Rudy Vallee, Decca 2551 (78)
When Winter Comes
Artie Shaw Orchestra (vocal by Tony Pastor),
Bluebird B10307 (78)

1940:

Berlin returned to Broadway with the show "Louisiana Purchase". Opening on May 28, 1940, this
featured Victor Moore, William Gaxton, Irene
Bordoni, Vera Zorina, Jim Taylor, and Carol Bruce,
later of Al Jolson's Colgate Radio Show. Berlin
score:

Dance With Me (At The Mardi Gras)
Wayne King Orchestra, Victor 26629 (78)
Fools Fall In Love
Charlie Barnet Orchestra (vocal by Mary Ann
McCall), Bluebird B-10691 (78)
Joan Edwards (vocal and piano), Liberty Music
Shop L-304 (78)
Shirley Howard, Bluebird B-10724 (78)
Tony Martin, Decca 3175 (78)
I'd Love To Be Shot From A Cannon With You
It'll Come To You
Shirley Howard, Bluebird B-10724 (78)
Leo Reisman Orchestra (vocal by Anita Boyer),
Victor 26579 (78)
It's A Lovely Day Tomorrow
Sung by Irene Bordoni.
Chick Bullock, Vocalion 5583 (78)

Tommy Dorsey Orchestra (vocal by Frank Sinatra), Victor 26596 (78)

Mary Martin, Columbia 4566-M [Album MM-843] (78)

Jan Savitt Orchestra (vocal by Allan DeWitt, Decca 3178 (78)

Bea Wain, Victor 26580 (78)

Latins Know How

Sung by Irene Bordoni.

Joan Edwards (vocal and piano), Liberty Music Shop L-304 (78)

Leo Reisman Orchestra (vocal by Anita Boyer), Victor 26579 (78)

The Lord Done Fixed Up My Soul

Sung by Carol Bruce.

Jan Savitt Orchestra (vocal by Allan DeWitt), Decca 3177 (78)

Louisiana Purchase

Sung by Carol Bruce.

Hal Kemp Orchestra (with vocal chorus), Victor 26592 (78)

Old Man's Darling, Young Man's Slave

Outside Of That I Love You

Dinah Shore and Barry Wood, Bluebird [catalogue number unknown] (78)

Sex Marches On

Sung by Jim Taylor.

Tonight At The Mardi Gras

What Chance Have I With Love

Wild About You

You Can't Brush Me Off

Hal Kemp Orchestra (with vocal chorus), Victor 26592 (78)

Jan Savitt Orchestra (vocal by Allen DeWitt), Decca 3178 (78)

You're Lonely And I'm Lonely

Charlie Barnet Orchestra (vocal by Mary Ann McCall), Bluebird B-10691 (78)
Chick Bullock, Vocalion 5583 (78)
Tommy Dorsey Orchestra (vocal by Frank Sinatra), Victor 26596 (78)
Mary Martin, Decca 23151 (78)
Tony Martin, Decca 2175 (78)
Jan Savitt Orchestra (vocal by Allan DeWitt), Decca 3177 (78)

1941 (as war clouds gathered):

Any Bonds Today?
Title phrase melodically identical with phrase "Any yam today?" from Berlin's 1938 "The Yam". All royalties donated to U.S. Treasury Dept.
Andrews Sisters, Decca 4044 (78)
Jimmy Dorsey Orchestra (vocal by Helen O'Connell and Bob Eberle), Decca 4044 (78)
Kay Kyser Orchestra (with vocal chorus), Columbia 36228 (78)
Barry Wood (with Lyn Murray Singers), Victor 27478 (78)
A Little Old Church In England
Glenn Miller Orchestra (vocal by Ray Eberle, Dorothy Clare, and Modernaires), Bluebird B11069 (78)

The film version of "Louisiana Purchase" was made a Bob Hope comedy with Hope supported by Vera Zorina, Victor Moore, Irene Bordoni, Donna Drake, Raymond Walburn, and Maxie Rosenbloom. Only four Berlin numbers were retained from the show, and of these, "Dance With Me (At The Mardi Gras)" and "It's A Lovely Day Tomorrow" were deleted.

89

It's New To Us
  Opening Number written especially for the film
  version by Irving Berlin.
Louisiana Purchase
  Sung by Vera Zorina with Chorus and Dance
  Ensemble.
You're Lonely And I'm Lonely
  Sung by Irene Bordoni and Victor Moore.

1942:

Angels Of Mercy
  All royalties donated to American Red Cross.
  Bing Crosby, Australian Decca Y5771 (78) [un-
  issued in U.S.]
  Glen Gray and Casa Loma Orchestra (vocal by
  Kenny Sargent), Decca 4170 (78)
  Glenn Miller Orchestra (vocal by Ray Eberle
  and Chorus), Bluebird B11429 (78)
  Fred Waring's Pennsylvanians, Decca 18280 (78)
Arms For The Love Of America
  All royalties donated to Army Ordinance Dept.
  Kay Kyser Orchestra (with vocal chorus), Col-
  umbia 36228 (78)
  Barry Wood (with Lyn Murray Singers), Victor
  27478 (10") (78)
  Barry Wood (with Lyn Murray Singers), Victor
  36404 (12") (78)
I Paid My Income Tax Today
  All royalties donated to U.S. Treasury Dept.
  Dick Robertson (vocal) and his Orchestra, Decca
  4151 [Album A-253] (78)
  Barry Wood, Victor 27760 (78)
I Threw A Kiss In The Ocean
  All royalties donated to U.S. Navy Relief.

Jimmy Dorsey Orchestra (vocal by Helen O'Connell),
Decca 4304 (78)
Benny Goodman Orchestra (with vocal chorus),
Columbia 36590 (78)
Horace Heidt and Musical Knights (with vocal
chorus), Columbia 36568 (78)
Kate Smith, Columbia 36552 (78)
The President's Birthday Ball
All royalties donated to National Foundation for
Infantile Paralysis.
Jimmy Dorsey Orchestra (vocal by Bob Eberle),
Decca 4170 (78)
Glenn Miller Orchestra (vocal by Marion Hutton
and Modernaires), Bluebird B11429 (78)
Barry Wood, Victor 27760 (78)
Me And My Melinda
Jimmy Dorsey Orchestra (vocal by Phil Washburn),
Decca 4263 (78)
Kay Kyser Orchestra (with vocal chorus), Col-
umbia 36558 (78)
When That Man Is Dead And Gone
Glenn Miller Orchestra (vocal by Tex Beneke
and Modernaires), Bluebird B11069 (78)
When This Crazy World Is Sane Again

On July 4, 1942, during a second World War, Irving
Berlin's second revue for Army Emergency Relief
opened at the Century Theatre: "This Is The Army".
In the cast were 300 G.I.s including William
Horne, Chester O'Brien, Kenneth Bates, Dick
Bernie, Leonard Berchman, Burl Ives, Anthony
Ross, Robert Moore, Orlando Johnson, Ralph Magels-
sen, Roger Kinne; Privates Jules Oshins, Gary
Merrill (as Interlocutor), Tileston Perry, Alan
Manson, Stuart Churchill, Robert Shanley; Privates
First Class Joe Cook Jr., James McColl; Corporals

Philip Truex, Nelson Barclift, Earl Oxford, James
("Stump") Cross; Sergeant Hayden Rorke, Staff
Sergeant Ezra Stone, and, this time a civilian,
Mr. Irving Berlin. Additional to the new score,
"Mandy" and "Oh! How I Hate To Get Up In The
Morning" were revived from "Yip, Yip, Yaphank",
the latter again sung by Berlin in a scene nos-
talgically played by other veterans of the original show. Numbers sung on stage by same performers
as in original cast album (which, incidentally,
was released nineteen catalogue numbers before
the alleged "first" original cast album, "Okla-
homa!"). Berlin score:

MEDLEY (a) American Eagles
       (b) With My Head In The Clouds
          Kay Kyser Orchestra (with vocal chorus),
          V-Disc 96 (12") (78)
The Army's Made A Man Out Of Me
How About A Cheer For The Navy?
I Left My Heart At The Stage Door Canteen
  Kenny Baker, Decca 18442 (78)
  Russ Morgan (vocal) and his Orchestra, Decca
  18444 (78)
  Charlie Spivak Orchestra (with vocal chorus),
  Columbia 36620 (78)
I'm Getting Tired So I Can Sleep
  Kenny Baker, Decca 18442 (78)
  Jimmy Dorsey Orchestra (vocal by Bob Eberle),
  Decca 18462 (78)
  Claude Thornhill Orchestra (with vocal chorus),
  Columbia 36658 (78)
  Victor "First Nighter" Orchestra (vocal by
  Brad Reynolds and Male Chorus), Victor 27956
  [Album P-131] (78)
  Barry Wood, Bluebird B11572 (78)

Ladies Of The Chorus
Mandy
   With Private Richard Irving as Mandy.
My Sergeant And I
Oh! How I Hate To Get Up In The Morning
   Irving Berlin (May 7, 1947), V-Disc 780 (12")
   (78)
   Arthur Fields, Victor 18489 (78)
   Arthur Fields, Columbia A2617 (78)
A Soldier's Dream
That Russian Winter
   Sung by Private Jules Oshins.
   Ray McKinley (vocal) and his Orchestra, Cap-
   itol 128 (78)
   Russ Morgan (vocal) and his Orchestra, Decca
   18444 (78)
This Is The Army, Mister Jones
   Irving Berlin (with the Original Chorus and
   Orchestra), British HMV B.9355 (78)
   Horace Heidt and his Musical Knights, Columbia
   36667 (78)
What The Well-Dressed Man In Harlem Will Wear
   Victor "First Nighter" Orchestra (vocal by
   Thomas "Fats" Waller with Male Chorus), Victor
   27956 [Album P-131] (78)
This Time (Is The Last Time)
   Finale - sung by Entire Cast of 300.
   Dick Robertson (vocal) and his Orchestra,
   Decca 4318 (78)
   Kate Smith, Columbia 36540 (78)

In addition to the following original cast album,
another album of eight selections from this show
was recorded in 78 rpm, Victor P-131 (Victor
27954-27957 inclusive) by The Victor "First Nighter" Orchestra; songs and various guest vocalists

<u>unknown.</u>

"THIS IS THE ARMY" MEDLEY
Szeth Myri, V-Disc 140 (12") (78)

This Is The Army, Mister Jones
I'm Getting Tired So I Can Sleep
I Left My Heart At The Stage Door Canteen

<u>following 78 rpm original cast album also pressed</u>
<u>on 33-1/3 rpm 10" 1p Decca DL-5108:</u>

IRVING BERLIN'S All-Soldier Show
THIS IS THE ARMY
Recorded by the Original All-Soldier Cast
Decca A-340

<u>Decca 18474</u>

OVERTURE

This Is The Army, Mister Jones
I Left My Heart At The Stage Door Canteen
That Russian Winter
(All Soldier Orchestra and Chorus, Under the Dir-
ection of Corporal Milton Rosenstock)

I Left My Heart At The Stage Door Canteen
(Corporal Earl Oxford and Soldier Chorus)

<u>Decca 18475</u>

The Army's Made A Man Out Of Me
(Staff Sergeant Ezra Stone, Corporal Philip
Truex, Private Julie Oshins)

I'm Getting Tired So I Can Sleep
(Private Stuart Churchill and Soldier Octet)

Decca 18476

MEDLEY

American Eagles
With My Head In The Clouds
(Private Robert Shanley and Soldier Chorus)

What The Well-Dressed Man In Harlem Will Wear
(Corporal James "Stump" Cross with All Soldier
Swing Band)

Decca 18477

Oh! How I Hate To Get Up In The Morning
(Mr. Irving Berlin with a Supporting Cast and
Soldier Chorus)

How About A Cheer For The Navy?
(All Soldier Orchestra and Chorus Under the Direction of Corporal Milton Rosenstock)

Earlier in 1942 came the Bing Crosby-Fred Astaire
film "Holiday Inn". Besides reviving "Lazy" and
"Easter Parade", Berlin met the challenge he'd set
for himself (originally conceived for a stage
musical) to write a song for each of the major
American holidays. Numbers sung in film mostly
by same artists as in original cast album. Berlin
score:

Abraham   (for Lincoln's Birthday)
   Sung by Bing Crosby (with Negro Choir).

Carol Bruce, V-Disc 87 (12") (78)
Freddy Martin Orchestra (vocal by Glenn Hughes),
Victor 27946 (78)
Be Careful, It's My Heart
Sung by Bing Crosby. For St. Valentine's Day.
Tommy Dorsey Orchestra (vocal by Frank Sinatra),
Victor 27923 (78); RCA Camden CAL-650 (33-1/3)
Connie Haines, Capitol 114 (78)
Russ Morgan, MGM E4240 (33-1/3)
Dinah Shore, Victor 27940 (78)
Frank Sinatra, Reprise F-1001 (33-1/3)
Kate Smith, Columbia 36618 (78)
Dick Stabile Orchestra, Decca 4351 (78)
Claude Thornhill Orchestra, Columbia 36616 (78)
Easter Parade
Sung by Bing Crosby. For Easter.

MEDLEY (a) Happy Holiday
(b) Come To Holiday Inn
Sung by Bing Crosby.
I Can't Tell A Lie
Sung and danced by Fred Astaire. For Washington
Birthday.
I'll Capture Your Heart
Opening Number sung and danced by Bing Crosby
and Fred Astaire with Marjorie Reynolds; re-
prised by same performers (different lyrics) for
Finale.
I've Got Plenty To Be Thankful For.
Sung by Bing Crosby. For Thanksgiving Day.
Lazy
Sung by Bing Crosby
Let's Start The New Year Right.
Sung by Bing Crosby; eight bars reprised (by
Ensemble) for Finale. For New Years' Day.
Say It With Firecrackers.

An instrumental, danced by Fred Astaire to
firecracker accompaniment. For 4th of July.
Song Of Freedom
    Sung by Bing Crosby. Writter for 4th of July,
    but withdrawn in favor of the above.
You're Easy To Dance With
    Sung and danced by Fred Astaire; one line
    reprised by Astaire for Finale.
    Fred Astaire (1960), Verve V-2114 (33-1/3)
    Dick Stabile Orchestra, Decca 4351 (78)
White Christmas
    Sung by Bing Crosby. For Christmas. Winner
    of Academy Award (Oscar) Best Song Written For
    A Motion Picture, 1942.
    Louis Armstrong (vocal) and his Orchestra,
    Decca 28443 (78)
    Army Air Force Training Center Band (medley),
    V-Disc 388 (12") (78)
    Ames Brothers, Coral 60013 (78)
    Eddy Arnold, RCA Victor 21-0390 (78)
    Phil Brito, MGM 10779 (78)
    Carmen Cavallaro (piano), Decca 24141 (78)
    Jesse Crawford (organ), Decca 24143 (78)
    Bing Crosby (1944), V-Disc 441 (12") (78)
    Bing Crosby (1947), V-Disc 797 (12") (78)
    Vic Damone, Mercury 5178 (78); Mercury 5515x45
    (45)
    DePaul Choristers, Columbia B-725 (45) (ep)
    Gracie Fields, London 30133 (78)
    Eddie Fisher (with Chorus), RCA Victor LPM-
    3065 (33-1/3)
    Eddie Fisher (medley), RCA Victor LOC-1024
    (33-1/3)
    Ken Griffin (organ), Columbia B-6923 (45) (ep)
    Jascha Heifitz (violin), Decca 23376 (78); Decca
    DL-38016 (33-1/3)

Ink Spots, Decca 24140 (78)
Harry James Orchestra, Columbia 37955 (78)
Gordon Jenkins Orchestra (vocal by Bob Carroll),
Capitol 124/1263/15202 (78)
Mahalia Jackson, Columbia B-702 (45) (ep)
Guy Lombardo and his Royal Canadians, Decca
23738/Decca 28409 (78)
Dean Martin, Capitol T-1285 (33-1/3)
Freddy Martin Orchestra (vocal by Clyde Rogers),
Victor 27946 (78) *
Barry O'Dowd, Australian Planet PP-001 (33-1/3)
Elvis Presley, RCA Victor LPM-1951 (33-1/3); RCA
Victor EPA-4340 (45) (ep)
Artie Shaw Orchestra, Decca 27243 (78)
Dinah Shore, RCA Victor 45-0009 (78)
Frank Sinatra (1944), Columbia 36756/36860/
37152/38257 (78) *
Frank Sinatra (1946), V-Disc 652 (12") (78)
Frank Sinatra (1947), British Columbia D.B.
3745 (78) [unissued in U.S.]
Frank Sinatra (1954), Capitol 2954 (78)
Ethel Smith (console organ), Decca 24142 (78)
Kate Smith, MGM 10096 (78)
Charlie Spivak Orchestra, V-Disc 295 (12") (78)
Charlie Spivak Orchestra, Columbia 36649 (78)
Jo Stafford (with Lyn Murray Singers), Capitol
319/1262/15200 (78)
Sister Rosetta Tharpe, Decca 48119 (78)
Three Suns, RCA Victor EPA-655 (45) (ep)
Ernest Tubb, Decca 46183 (78)
Wesley Tuttle, Capitol 1266/Capitol 15206 (78)
Fred Waring's Pennsylvanians, Decca 24500 (78)
Fred Waring's Pennsylvanians, Reprise F-2022
(33-1/3)
Hugo Winterhalter Orchestra and Chorus, Victor
20-3937 (78)

The following 78 rpm original cast album has been pressed on 33-1/3 rpm 12" lp Decca DL-4256 (Bing's Hollywood - Holiday Inn), still available. It was also released in 78 rpm, Decca A-534 (Decca 23820-23823 inclusive) and on 33-1/3 rpm 10" lp Decca DL-5092, by the deletion of Bing Crosby's "Easter Parade" and "I've Got Plenty To Be Thankful For" (coupled on single Decca 23819), "Lazy", and "White Christmas". The latter, included in Decca Album A-403 (Decca 18429; c/w "Let's Start The New Year Right") and Decca Album A-550 (Decca 23778; c/w "God Rest Ye Merry, Gentlemen"), in total sales of both the single and the "Merry Christmas" album, has reached a global sale of twenty-five million copies (the largest selling recording of all time). Another twenty-five million have been sold of "White Christmas" by all other recording artists combined. Grand Total: 50,000,000!

Song Hits From The Paramount Picture
HOLIDAY INN
BING CROSBY * FRED ASTAIRE
Decca A-306

Decca 18424

MEDLEY

Happy Holiday (a)   Come To Holiday Inn (b)
(Bing Crosby with The Music Maids and Hal)

Be Careful, It's My Heart
(Bing Crosby

Abraham
(Bing Crosby with Ken Darby Singers)

Easter Parade
(Bing Crosby)

Decca 18426

I've Got Plenty To Be Thankful For
(Bing Crosby)
Song Of Freedom
(Bing Crosby with Ken Darby Singers)

Decca 18427

I'll Capture Your Heart
(Bing Crosby and Fred Astaire with Margaret
Lenhart)

Lazy
(Bing Crosby)

Decca 18428

You're Easy To Dance With
(Fred Astaire)

I Can't Tell A Lie
(Fred Astaire)

Decca 18429

White Christmas
(Bing Crosby with Ken Darby Singers)

Let's Start The New Year Right
(Bing Crosby)

1943:

Berlin took "This Is The Army" on a nationwide
tour, culminating in Hollywood where it was filmed with Irving Berlin (again singing "Oh! How I
Hate To Get Up In The Morning", prompting an
unknown electrician who heard his sound-track
recording to sneer: "If the guy who wrote that
song could hear this guy sing it, he'd turn over
in his grave!"), future-Governor (then Lieutenant)
Ronald Reagan, future-Senator George Murphy, Joan
Leslie, George Tobias, Alan Hale, Charles Butter-
worth, Dolores Costello, Una Merkel, Ruth Donnelly,
Stanley Ridges, Rosemary DeCamp, Dorothy Peterson,
Frances Langford, Gertrude Neisen, Kate Smith,
plus Ezra Stone and others from the stage version.
Songs retained:

MEDLEY (a) American Eagles
       (b) With My Head In The Clouds
The Army's Made A Man Out Of Me
How About A Cheer For The Navy?
I Left My Heart At The Stage Door Canteen
I'm Getting Tired So I Can Sleep
Ladies Of The Chorus
Mandy
Oh! How I Hate To Get Up In The Morning
Poor Little Me - I'm On K. P.
  (also known as "Kitchen Police")
This Is The Army, Mister Jones
This Time
What The Well-Dressed Man In Harlem Will Wear

plus a tremendous guester by Kate Smith, bringing
the house down with "God Bless America"!

Then "This Is The Army" was taken overseas for a
tour of England, Ireland, and Scotland. For inter
polation into the overseas edition, Berlin wrote:

My British Buddy
  Irving Berlin (with the Original Chorus and Orch
  estra)*, British HMV B.9355 (78)
The Kick In The Pants
Ve Don't Like It
                    *(announcement by John Watt)

<u>1944:</u>

All Of My Life
  Bing Crosby, Decca 18658 (78)
  Harry James Orchestra, V-Disc 454 (12") (78)
  Kate Smith, Columbia 36783 (78)

The overseas tour of "This Is The Army" continued
through combat areas of Europe, the Near East,
and the Pacific. For interpolation into the
overseas edition, Berlin wrote:

The Fifth Army's Where My Heart Is
  A film-clip of Irving Berlin singing this for
  G.I.s in the Italian sector was shown on TV
  seventeen years later, "USO Wherever They Go!",
  October 8, 1961.
There Are No Wings On A Foxhole
What Are We Going To Do With All The Jeeps?

Everybody Knew But Me
  A previously unpublished number, actually written
  during 1940.
  Louis Prima Orchestra (vocal by Lilyann Carol),
  Majestic 7163 (78)
  Dinah Shore, RCA Victor 20-1798 (78)
Heaven Watch The Philipines
  Written when the United States granted indepen-
  dence to the Philipine Islands.
I'll Dance Rings Around You
Just A Blue Serge Suit
  Merry Macs, Decca 18715 (78)
Oh, To Be Home Again
The Race Horse And The Flea
Wilhelmina

1946:

The war over, Berlin now wrote what's supposed to
be his greatest score for the show "Annie, Get
Your Gun". Ethel Merman starred with Ray Middleton and George Lipton, William O'Neal, Harry
Bellaver, Robert Lenn, and Kathleen Carnes.
Numbers sung in show by same artists as in
original cast album. This musical comedy,
produced by Rodgers & Hammerstein, was originally to have been scored by Jerome Kern under the
title "Annie Oakley". Kern's untimely death
resulted in the following Berlin score:

Ballyhoo
Anything You Can Do
  (Better known as "Anything You Can Do I Can
  Do Better")

Sung by Ethel Merman and Ray Middleton.
Bing Crosby, Dick Haymes, Andrews Sisters,
Decca 40039 [Album A-628] (78)
Colonel Buffalo Bill
  Sung by William O'Neal and Ensemble.
Doin' What Comes Natur'lly
  Sung by Ethel Merman with Garth, Turner, and
  Bibb.
  Jimmy Dorsey Orchestra (with vocal chorus),
  Decca 18872/Decca 25487 (78)
  Freddy Martin Orchestra (vocal by Glenn Hughes
  and Martin Men), RCA Victor 20-1878 (78)
  Ethel Merman (medley) (1962), Reprise R-6062
  (33-1/3)
  Dinah Shore, Columbia 36976 (78)
The Girl That I Marry
  Sung by Ray Middleton.
  Ray Anthony Orchestra, Capitol 1020 (78)
  Eddie Fisher, RCA Victor LPM-1097 (33-1/3)
  Dick Haymes, Decca 23780/Decca 27518 (78)
  Frank Sinatra, Columbia 36875 (78); Columbia CL-
  1136/CL-1297 (33-1/3)
  Frank Sinatra, V-Disc 679 (12") (78)
  Frank Sinatra (conducting orchestra), Reprise
  9-6045 (33-1/3)
I Got Lost In His Arms
  Sung by Ethel Merman (with Chorus).
  Jane Froman, Majestic 1049 (78); Royale 254
  (45) (ep)
  Marie Greene, V-Disc 670 (12") (78)
  Judy Holliday, Columbia CL-1153 (33-1/3)
  Leo Reisman Orchestra, Decca 18861 (78)
  Dinah Shore, Columbia 36976 (78)
I Got The Sun In The Morning
  Sung by Ethel Merman (with Chorus)
  Les Brown and his Band of Renown, Columbia 36977 (78)

Dean Martin, Diamond 2036 (78)
Ethel Merman (medley) (1962), Reprise R-6062
(33-1/3)
Leo Reisman Orchestra, Decca 18861 (78)
Artie Shaw Orchestra, MGM 10730 (78); MGM
E4240 (33-1/3)
I'll Share It All With You
  Sung by Kathleen Carnes and Robert Lenn.
I'm A Bad, Bad Man
  Sung by Ray Middleton (with Chorus)
I'm An Indian Too
  Sung by Ethel Merman (with Chorus).
Let's Go West Again
  Withdrawn from show. Four years later, Judy
  Garland recorded this for the sound track of
  "Annie, Get Your Gun", leading to the supposition
  that it was written for the film. It was
  dropped from the film version in 1950, but had
  already been dropped from the stage version in
  1946.
Al Jolson, Decca 24905 (78); Decca DL-5014
(10")/Decca DL-9037 (12") (33-1/3)
Eddy Duchin (piano), Columbia 38740 (78)
Sons Of The Pioneers, RCA Victor 21-0171 (78);
RCA Victor 48-0184 (45)
Moonshine Lullaby
  Sung by Ethel Merman with Garth, Turner, and
  Bibb.
My Defenses Are Down
  Sung by Ray Middleton (with Male Chorus)
Take It In Your Stride
  Withdrawn from show.
(There's No Business Like) Show Business
  Written to fill a stage-wait, this proved to be
  the show's most durable hit.
Eddie Cantor, Audio Fidelity AFLP-702 (33-1/3)

Bing Crosby, Dick Haymes, Andrews Sisters,
Decca 40039 [Album A-628] (78)
Ethel Merman (June 15, 1953), Decca DL-7027
(33-1/3)
Ethel Merman and Mary Martin (medley), Decca
DL- 7027 (33-1/3)
Ethel Merman (sound-track), Decca 29379 (10")/
Decca 90057 (12") (78)
Ethel Merman (1962), Reprise R-6062 (33-1/3)
Artie Shaw Orchestra, MGM 10730 (78)
Blossom Seeley and Benny Fields, Mercury MG-
20224 (33-1/3)
Frank Sinatra, Columbia 38829 (78); Columbia
CL-1297 (33-1/3)
Mel Torme and Mel-Tones, Musicraft 15111 (78)
They Say It's Wonderful
Sung by Ethel Merman and Ray Middleton.
Ray Anthony Orchestra, Capitol 1020 (78)
Eileen Barton, Mercury 5410 (78)
Vivian Blaine, Mercury MG-20234 (33-1/3)
Perry Como, RCA Victor 20-1857 (78)
Bing Crosby, Decca 18829/Decca 18846/Decca
27277 (78)
Allan Jones, RCA Victor 10-1541 (78); RCA
Victor 49-1167 (45)
Gordon MacRae, MGM 10734 (78)
Ethel Merman (1962), Reprise R-6062 (33-1/3)
Andy Russell, Capitol 1096 (78)/Capitol 252 (78
Frank Sinatra, Columbia 36975 (78); Columbia CL
1297 (33-1/3)
Frank Sinatra, V-Disc 670 (12") (78)
Jerry Wald Orchestra (vocal by Anne Russell),
Sonora 3007 (78)
Who Do You Love, I Hope?
Sung by Kethleen Carnes and Robert Lenn.

Georgie Price with Betty Johnston, Stork ST-
1010 (78)
Andy Russell, Capitol 271 (78)
With Music
Withdrawn from show.
You Can't Get A Man With A Gun
Sung by Ethel Merman.
Judy Garland, MGM E4005P/MGM E4240/Metro M-
581 (33-1/3)
Ethel Merman (1962), Reprise R-6062 (33-1/3)

The following 78 rpm original cast album was also
pressed on 33-1/3 rpm 12" lp's Decca DL-8001 (black
seal) and Decca DL-9018 (red seal), the latter
still available; in 45 rpm standard-play, Decca
Album 9-12 (Decca 9-23584 - 9-23589 inclusive) and
45 rpm extended-play, Decca Album ED-805 (Decca
91211 - 91213 inclusive).

ETHEL MERMAN
In the Richard Rodgers -
Oscar Hammerstein II Production
ANNIE GET YOUR GUN
Music and Lyrics by IRVING BERLIN

Decca A-468

Decca 23584

Doin' What Comes Natur'lly
(Ethel Merman)

Moonshine Lullaby
(Ethel Merman with Garth, Turner, and Bibb)

Decca 23585

You Can't Get A Man With A Gun
(Ethel Merman)

I'm An Indian Too
(Ethel Merman with Chorus)

Decca 23586

They Say It's Wonderful
(Ethel Merman and Ray Middleton)

Anything You Can Do
(Ethel Merman and Ray Middleton)

Decca 23587

I Got Lost In His Arms
(Ethel Merman with Chorus)

I Got The Sun In The Morning
(Ethel Merman with Chorus)

Decca 23588

The Girl That I Marry
(Ray Middleton)

My Defenses Are Down
(Ray Middleton with Male Chorus)

Decca 23589

Who Do You Love, I Hope?
(Robert Lenn and Kathleen Carnes)

(There's No Business Like) Show Business
Annie Get Your Gun Chorus and Orchestra

An album of four 78 rpm discs of selections from
this show was recorded by Al Goodman and his Orchestra (RCA Victor C-38) with Audrey Marsh and
Maxine Carroll (sopranos), Jimmy Carroll and Earl
Oxford (tenors), Mullen Sisters and Guild Choristers, including "They Say It's Wonderful", "I
Got Lost In His Arms", "You Can't Get A Man With
A Gun", "Doin' What Comes Natur'lly", "The Girl
That I Marry", "Who Do You Love, I Hope?", "Moonshine Lullaby", "I Got The Sun In The Morning".
Selections from "Annie Get Your Gun" were performed by someone named Coates on Side 1 of
33-1/3 rpm 12" lp RCA Camden CAL-154 c/w selections from "Miss Liberty". The following
33-1/3 rpm 12" lp, released during April, 1963,
is also of interest.

A Brilliant New Recording
Of Irving Berlin's Broadway Smash Hit
DORIS DAY * ROBERT GOULET
In
ANNIE GET YOUR GUN

Columbia OL-5960

Side 1:

OVERTURE

Show Business
The Girl That I Marry
I Got The Sun In The Morning
They Say It's Wonderful

Colonel Buffalo Bill (Leonard Stokes)
I'm A Bad, Bad Man (Robert Goulet)
Doin' What Comes Natur'lly (Doris Day)
The Girl That I Marry (Robert Goulet)
You Can't Get A Man With A Gun (Doris Day)
They Say It's Wonderful (Doris Day and Robert
  Goulet)
My Defenses Are Down (Robert Goulet)

Side 2:

Moonshine Lullaby (Doris Day)
I'm An Indian Too (Doris Day)
I Got Lost In His Arms (Doris Day)
Who Do You Love, I Hope? (Kelly Brown and Rennee
  Winters)
I Got The Sun In The Morning (Doris Day)
Anything You Can Do (Doris Day and Robert Goulet)
(There's No Business Like) Show Business (Ensemble

During 1946 came a second Bing Crosby Fred Astaire
film (featuring Joan Caulfield) and the second
Berlin filmusical primarily devoted to hits from
the past: "Blue Skies". Standards sung therein
and those who sang them, included: "All By Myself
(Bing Crosby), "Blue Skies" (Bing Crosby), "Heat
Wave" (Olga San Juan), "How Deep Is The Ocean?"
(Female Quartette), "I'll See You In C-U-B-A"
(Bing Crosby and Olga San Juan), "I've Got My
Captain Working For Me Now" (Bing Crosby and Billy
DeWolfe) (this sound-track recording was released
on V-Disc 820), "The Little Things In Life" (Bing
Crosby), "Not For All The Rice In China" (Bing
Crosby), "A Pretty Girl Is Like A Melody" (Male
Quartette), "Puttin' On The Ritz" (sung and danced
by Fred Astaire, with new lyrics by Berlin, in a

Production Number that proved to be the hit of the film), "Russian Lullaby" (Bing Crosby), "White Christmas" (Bing Crosby), "You'd Be Surprised" (Olga San Juan), not all of which were sung in full. Neither were all of the many others including "Always", "Any Bonds Today?", "Everybody Step", "This Is The Army, Mister Jones", etc. For this film, Berlin wrote only the following four new selections:

A Couple Of Song And Dance Men
    Sung and danced by Bing Crosby and Fred Astaire.
(Running Around In Circles) Getting Nowhere
    Sung by Bing Crosby.
A Serenade To An Old-Fashioned Girl
    Sung by Joan Caulfield.
You Keep Coming Back Like A Song
    Sung by Bing Crosby.
    Dennis Day, RCA Victor 20-1947 (78)
    Vera Massey, Diamond 2040 (78)
    Jo Stafford, Capitol 297 (78)

The following 78 rpm original cast album, by the deletion of Bing Crosby's "A Serenade To An Old-Fashioned Girl" and "Everybody Step", was pressed on 33-1/3 rpm 10" lp Decca DL-5042. By the deletion of only Fred Astaire's "Puttin' On The Ritz", and the addition of Crosby recordings of three selections from another film ("Out Of This World"), it was later pressed on 33-1/3 rpm 12" lp Decca DL-4259 ("Bing's Hollywood - "Blue Skies") still available.

Irving Berlin's BLUE SKIES
BING CROSBY * FRED ASTAIRE
Decca A-481

111

Decca 23646

Blue Skies (Bing Crosby with Choir)
I'll See You In C-U-B-A (Bing Crosby with Trudy
  Erwin)

Decca 23647

You Keep Coming Back Like A Song (Bing Crosby wit
  Quartette)
(Running Around In Circles) Getting Nowhere (Bing
  Crosby with Quartette)

Decca 23648

A Serenade To An Old-Fashioned Girl (Bing Crosby
  with Choir)
Everybody Step (Bing Crosby)

Decca 23649

All By Myself (Bing Crosby)
I've Got My Captain Working For Me Now (Bing
  Crosby)

Decca 23650

A Couple Of Song And Dance Men (Bing Crosby and
  Fred Astaire)
Puttin' On The Ritz (Fred Astaire)

1947:

The Friars gave a Roastmaster Dinner in honor of
Al Jolson for which Berlin wrote and sang an unpublished number kidding Al (title unknown), an

I have taken down some tributes for an old-time
pal,
The best that were on my shelf.
But there weren't any tributes I could pay to Al
That Al hasn't paid to himself.

Help Me To Help My Neighbor
Kenny Baker, Decca 14514 (78)
Kate (Have I Come Too Early, Too Late)
Hal Derwin Orchestra (vocal by Hi-Liters),
Capitol 467 (78)
Four Chicks and A Chuck, MGM 10048 (78)
Guy Lombardo and his Royal Canadians, Decca
23989 (78)
Love And The Weather
Kenny Baker (with Russ Morgan Orchestra),
Decca 24117 (78)
Dennis Day, RCA Victor 20-2360 (78)
Harry James Orchestra (vocal by Marion Morgan),
Columbia 37588 (78)
Jo Stafford, Capitol 443 (78)

1948:

The Freedom Train
All royalties donated to finance nationwide
tour of the Freedom Train.
Buddy Clark, Columbia 37889 (78)
Bing Crosby and Andrews Sisters, Decca 23999
(78)
Johnny Mercer, Peggy Lee, Benny Goodman,
Margaret Whiting, Pied Pipers (vocal) with
Paul Weston Orchestra, Capitol 15003 (78)
What Can You Do With A General

Featured in show "Stars On My Shoulders".
Resuscitated by Berlin for Bing Crosby to
"introduce" in 1954 film "White Christmas".
I Gave Her My Heart In Acapulco

"Easter Parade", Berlin's next filmusical (about
equally comprised of new and old numbers), was
to have starred Judy Garland and Gene Kelly.
Kelly broke a leg during rehearsals, however, and
was replaced by Fred Astaire (who co-starred with
Miss Garland three years later, in "The Lux Radio
Theatre" adaptation). Featured were Peter Law-
ford and Ann Miller. "The Girl On The Magazine
Cover" was sung by an unidentified baritone with
the air of a Prussian drillmaster; the many other
Berlin standards, and those who sang them, includ
ed: "Easter Parade" (Judy Garland), "I Love A
Piano" (Judy Garland), "I Want To Go Back To
Michigan (Down On The Farm)" (Judy Garland), "The
Ragtime Violin" (Fred Astaire), "Shaking The Blue
Away" (Ann Miller with Ensemble), "Snookey Ookums
(Judy Garland and Fred Astaire), "When The Mid-
night Choo-Choo Leaves For Alabam'" (Judy Garland
and Fred Astaire), and others. For this film,
Berlin wrote the following eight new selections:

Better Luck Next Time
  Sung by Judy Garland.
  Perry Como, RCA Victor 20-2888 (78)
  Jill Corey, Columbia CL-1095 (33-1/3)
  Judy Garland (sound-track), MGM E3149/MGM
  E3989P/MGM E4240 (33-1/3)
  Guy Lombardo and his Royal Canadians, Decca
  24435 (78)
  Jo Stafford, Capitol 15084 (78)

A Couple Of Swells
  Sung by Judy Garland and Fred Astaire. Later
  featured by Judy with various partners in
  vaudeville at the Palace, the Palladium, and
  other theatres.
Drum Crazy
  Sung and danced by Fred Astaire.
A Fella With An Umbrella
  Sung by Judy Garland and Peter Lawford.
  Bing Crosby, Decca 24433 (78)
  Skitch Henderson Orchestra, Capitol 15092 (78)
  Guy Lombardo and his Royal Canadians, Decca
  24434 (78)
  Frank Sinatra, Columbia 38192 (78)
Happy Easter
  Sung and danced by Fred Astaire.
It Only Happens When I Dance With You
  Sung by Fred Astaire; danced by Fred Astaire
  and Ann Miller.
  Fred Astaire (sound-track), MGM E4240 (33-1/3)
  Perry Como, RCA Victor 20-2888 (78)
  Vic Damone, Mercury 5166 (78)
  Guy Lombardo and his Royal Canadians, Decca
  24434 (78)
  Andy Russell, Capitol 15086 (78)
  Frank Sinatra, Columbia 38192 (78)
Mr. Monotony
  Judy Garland made a sound-track recording, but
  this song was dropped from the film. Berlin
  later resuscitated it for his 1949 show "Miss
  Liberty".
Steppin' Out With My Baby
  Sung and danced by Fred Astaire. Melody of
  release in chorus is same as release in chorus
  of Berlin's 1942 "The President's Birthday Ball".

Guy Lombardo and his Royal Canadians, Decca
24435 (78)
Gordon MacRae, Capitol 15091 (78)

following 78 rpm sound-track album also pressed on
33-1/3 rpm 10" lp MGM E-502:

Recorded Directly From The Sound Track
Of
The MGM Technicolor Musical

JUDY GARLAND · FRED ASTAIRE · Peter Lawford ·
Ann Miller

Irving Berlin's EASTER PARADE

MGM MGM-40

MGM 30185

Easter Parade (Judy Garland and Fred Astaire with
  Chorus)
A Fella With An Umbrella (Judy Garland and Peter
  Lawford)

MGM 30186

A Couple of Swells (Judy Garland and Fred Astaire)
  (a) I Love A Piano (Judy Garland)
  (b) Snookey Ookums (Judy Garland and Fred Astaire)
  (c) When The Midnight Choo-Choo Leaves For
      Alabam' (Judy Garland and Fred Astaire)

MGM 30187

Better Luck Next Time (Judy Garland)

It Only Happens When I Dance With You (Fred
    Astaire)

                    MGM 30188

Steppin' Out With My Baby (Fred Astaire with
    Chorus)
Shaking The Blues Away (Ann Miller with Chorus)

                    1949:

I'm Beginning To Miss You
    On Petrillo's recording ban being lifted, Berlin
    dashed this off in an hour.
    Doris Day, Columbia 38405 (78)
    Gordon Jenkins Orchestra and Chorus, Decca
    24593 (78)
    Bill Lawrence, RCA Victor 20-3355 (78)
    Andy Russell and King Sisters, Capitol 15388
    (78)
A Man Chases A Girl (Until She Catches Him)
    Resuscitated by Berlin for Donald O'Connor to
    "introduce" in 1954 film "There's No Business
    Like Show Business".
    Eddie Fisher (assisted by Debbie Reynolds),
    RCA Victor 20-6015 (78)
    Donald O'Connor, Decca 90059 (12") (78)

Irving Berling now wrote all songs for the show
"Miss Liberty". In the cast were Eddie Albert,
Allyn McLerie, Mary McCarty, Charles Dingle,
Philip Berghof, Ethel Griffies, and Herbert
Bourneuf. Numbers sung in show by same artists
as in original cast album. Berlin score:

                    117

Business For A Good Girl Is Bad
Extra! Extra!
Falling Out Of Love Can Be Fun
   Sung by Mary McCarty.
Follow The Leader Jig
Give Me Your Tired, Your Poor
   Finale - sung by Allyn McLerie and Ensemble.
   As a four-year-old immigrant, Irving Berlin's
   first sight of America must have been the
   Statue of Liberty. The words inscribed on
   the base of that statue - the lyrics of this
   song - are by Emma Lazarus.
   Tony Martin, RCA Victor 20-3535 (78); RCA
   Victor 47-3024 (45)
   Fred Waring's Pennsylvanians, Reprise F-2020
   (33-1/3)
Homework
   Sung by Mary McCarty.
   Andrews Sisters, Decca 24660 (78); Decca DL-
   5264 (33-1/3)
   Helen Forrest, MGM 10473 (78)
   Dinah Shore, Columbia 38514 (78)
   Jo Stafford, Capitol 57-665 (78)
   Fran Warren, RCA Victor 20-3466 (78); RCA
   Victor 47-2929 (78)
The Hon'rable Profession Of The Fourth Estate
I'd Like My Picture Took
   (title sometimes incorrectly given as "What
   Do I Have To Do To Get My Picture In The
   Papers?")
   Sung by Mary McCarty.
(Just One Way To Say) I Love You
   Sung by Eddie Albert and Allyn McLerie.
   Al Jolson, Decca 24665 (78); Decca DL-5314
   (10")/Decca DL-9037 (12") (33-1/3)
   Johnny Bradford, Bluebird 31-0010 (78)

Perry Como, RCA Victor 20-3469 (78); RCA Victor
47-2931 (45)
Billy Eckstine, MGM 10472 (78)
Patti Page, Mercury 5310 (78)
Frank Sinatra, Columbia 38513 (78)
Jo Stafford, Capitol 57-665 (78)
Let's Take An Old-Fashioned Walk
Sung by Eddie Albert and Allyn McLerie.
Johnny Bradford, Bluebird 31-0010 (78)
Perry Como, RCA Victor 20-3469 (78); RCA Victor
47-2931 (45)
Dick Haymes, Decca 24666 (78)
Frankie Masters, MGM 10465 (78)
Frank Sinatra and Doris Day, Columbia 38513
(78)
Margaret Whiting, Capitol 57-666 (78)
Little Fish In A Big Pond
Sung by Eddie Albert and Mary McCarty.
Buddy Clark and Dinah Shore, Columbia 38515
(78)
Dick Haymes, Decca 24666 (78)
Bill Lawrence, RCA Victor 20-3470 (78); RCA
Victor 47-2932 (45)
Me An' My Bundle
Buddy Clark, Columbia 38548 (78)
Miss Liberty
Mr. Monotony
The Most Expensive Statue In The World
Only For Americans
Sung by Ethel Griffies.
Andrews Sisters, Decca 24660 (78); Decca DL-
5264 (33-1/3)
Ray McKinley Orchestra, RCA Victor 20-3507
(78); RCA Victor 47-2979 (45)
Paris Wakes Up And Smiles
Sung by Johnny Thompson.

Al Jolson, Decca 24665 (78); Decca DL-5314
(10")/Decca DL-9037 (12") (33-1/3)
Buddy Clark, Columbia 38515 (78)
Jean Sablon, RCA Victor 20-3473 (78); RCA
Victor 47-2935 (45)
Margaret Whiting, Capitol 57-666 (78)
The Policemen's Ball
Sung by Mary McCarty.
The Train
You Can Have Him
Sung by Mary McCarty and Allyn McLerie.
Helen Forrest, MGM 10473 (78)
Peggy Lee, Capitol 57-670 (78)
Dinah Shore and Doris Day, Columbia 38514 (78)
Fran Warren, RCA Victor 20-3466 (78); RCA Victⓘ
47-2929 (45)
Eve Young, Bluebird 31-0009 (78)

following 78 rpm original cast album also pressed
on 33-1/3 rpm 12" lp Columbia ML-4220:

Original Broadway Cast

MISS LIBERTY

Columbia MM-860

Columbia 4572-M

OVERTURE-(a) Let's Take An Old-Fashioned Walk;
(b) The Policemen's Ball; (c) Little Fish In A
Big Pond; (d) I Love You; (e) Only For Americans
  ("Miss Liberty" Orchestra under the direction
  of Jay Blackton)
Give Me Your Tired, Your Poor (Allyn McLerie)

Columbia 4573-M

I'd Like My Picture Took (Mary McCarty)
The Most Expensive Statue In The World (Ensemble)
Falling Out Of Love Can Be Fun (Mary McCarty)

Columbia 4574-M

Little Fish In A Big Pond (Eddie Albert and Mary
     McCarty)
The Policemen's Ball (Mary McCarty and Chorus)

Columbia 4575-M

Let's Take An Old-Fashioned Walk (Eddie Albert,
     Allyn McLerie, and Chorus)
You Can Have Him (Mary McCarty and Allyn McLerie)

Columbia 4576-M

Homework (Mary McCarty)
(Just One Way To Say) I Love You (Eddie Albert
     and Allyn McLerie)

Columbia 4577-M

Paris Wakes Up And Smiles (Johnny Thompson and
     Chorus)
Only For Americans (Ethel Griffies and Chorus)

An album of four 78 rpm discs of selections from
this show was recorded by Al Goodman and his
Orchestra (Bluebird BN-4) including (vocalists'
names in parenthesis): "Little Fish In A Big
Pond" (Wynn Murray and Bob Wright), "Let's Take

121

An Old-Fashioned Walk" (Martha and Bob Wright and
Guild Choristers), "Homework" (Wynn Murray), "Paris
Wakes Up And Smiles" (Jimmy Carroll and Guild
Choristers), "Only For Americans" (Sondra Deal and
Guild Choristers), "(Just One Way To Say) I Love
You" (Martha and Bob Wright), "You Can Have Him"
(Wynn Murray and Martha Wright), "Give Me Your
Tired, Your Poor" (Martha Wright and Guild Chor-
isters). Selections from "Miss Liberty" were
performed by someone named Coates on Side 2 of
33-1/3 rpm 12" 1p RCA Camden CAL-154 c/w selections
from "Annie Get Your Gun". The following 33-1/3
rpm 10" 1p (also pressed on four 78 rpm discs,
Decca Album A-717) is of similar interest.

MISS LIBERTY

Fred Waring And The Pennsylvanians

Selections From The Musical Production

Decca DL-5009

Side 1:

(Just One Way To Say) I Love You
Little Fish In A Big Pond
Let's Take An Old-Fashioned Walk
The Policemen's Ball

Side 2:

Homework
You Can Have Him
Paris Wakes Up And Smiles

1950:

Irving Berlin next wrote all songs for the show
"Call Me Madam". Starred was Ethel Merman,
supported by Paul Lucas, Russell Nype, Galina
Talva, Jay Velie, Pat Harrington, and Ralph
Chambers. Numbers performed in show (except as
indicated in following notes) by same artists
as in original cast albums. Berlin score:

The Best Thing For You
    Sung by Ethel Merman.
    Russ Case Orchestra, MGM 10845 (78)
    Perry Como, RCA Victor 20-3922 (78)
    Bing Crosby, Decca 27250 (78); Decca DL-5298
    (33-1/3)
    Doris Day, Columbia 39008 (78)
    Eddie Fisher, RCA Victor LPM-1647 (33-1/3)
    Joyce India, Mercury 27250 (78)
    Margaret Whiting, Capitol 1213 (78)
Can You Use Any Money Today?
    Sung by Ethel Merman.
Free
    This number, the big flag-waving finale for
    Act Two, was withdrawn from "Call Me Madam"
    before the Broadway opening, when it failed to
    register with a Philadelphia audience. ("The
    public," Berlin says, "is never wrong.") At
    this time, Bing Crosby and his son
    Gary were selling a million of Berlin's 1914
    hit "Play A Simple Melody", suggesting to
    Berlin that "Free" might best be replaced by
    another counter-melody duet. [This proved to

be the hit of the show, "(I Wonder Why) You're Just In Love" (see below).] Berlin again used the melody of "Free" in its entirety, for a new lyric, "Snow", introduced in his 1954 film "White Christmas". The original "Free" was finally introduced on TV, November 14, 1955, by John Raitt.

The Hostess With The Mostes' On The Ball
  Sung by Ethel Merman.
  Ethel Merman (medley) (1962), Reprise R-6062 (33-1/3)

It's A Lovely Day Today
  Sung by Russell Nype and Galina Talva.
  Russ Case Orchestra, MGM 10833 (78)
  Perry Como and Fontaine Sisters, RCA Victor 20-3945 (78)

Marrying For Love
  Sung by Ethel Merman and Paul Lucas.
  Russ Case Orchestra, MGM 10833 (78)
  Rosemary Clooney and Guy Mitchell, Columbia 39052 (78)
  Perry Como, RCA Victor 20-3922 (78)
  Bing Crosby, Decca 27250 (78); Decca DL-5298 (33-1/3)

Mrs. Sally Adams
  Opening number; sung by Jay Blackton Chorus.

(Dance To The Music Of) The Ocarina
  Sung by Galina Talva.

Once Upon A Time Today
  Sung by Russell Nype.

Something To Dance About
  Sung by Ethel Merman.

They Like Ike
  Sung by Pat Harrington, Ralph Chambers, and Jay Velie.

Washington Square Dance

Sung by Ethel Merman.
Welcome To Lichtenburg
  (better known as "Lichtenburg")
  Sung by Paul Lucas.
(I Wonder Why) You're Just In Love
  Sung as a counter-melody duet by Ethel Merman
  and Russell Nype.
  Louis Armstrong and Velma Middleton, Decca
  27481 (78)
  Russ Case Orchestra, MGM 10845 (78)
  Rosemary Clooney and Guy Mitchell, Columbia
  39052 (78)
  Perry Como and Fontaine Sisters, RCA Victor
  20-3945 (78)
  Dancing Voices, MGM E4240 (33-1/3)
  Mary and Larry Martin, Columbia 39115 (78)
  Ethel Merman (medley), Decca DL-7027 (33-1/3)

Even though RCA Victor obtained exclusive rights
to record the original cast album, the star,
Ethel Merman, was under contract to Decca, and
Decca refused to loan her out. Instead, they
issued their own "original cast" album, wherein
the loud-voiced Miss Merman was supported by Dick
Haymes, Eileen Wilson, Gordon Jenkins' Orchestra
and Chorus. This, the following 78 rpm album,
was also pressed on 33-1/3 rpm 12" lp's Decca
DL-8035 (black seal) and Decca DL-9022 (red seal),
the latter still available; in 45 rpm standard
play, Decca Album 9-166 (Decca 9-27353-9-27358
inclusive). By the deletion of Ethel Merman's
"The Hostess With The Mostes' On The Ball" and
"Can You Use Any Money Today?", Gordon Jenkins'
"Welcome to Lichtenburg" and "They Like Ike",
this was also pressed on 33-1/3 rpm 10" lp
Decca DL-5304.

ETHEL MERMAN

12 Songs From CALL ME MADAM

Words and Music by IRVING BERLIN

Decca A-818

Decca 27353

The Hostess With The Mostes' On The Ball (Ethel
   Merman)
Can You Use Any Money Today? (Ethel Merman)

Decca 27354

The Best Thing For You (Ethel Merman with Chorus)
Marrying For Love (Ethel Merman with Chorus)

Decca 27355

(I Wonder Why) You're Just In Love (Ethel Merman
   and Dick Haymes with Chorus)
Something To Dance About (Ethel Merman with Chorus)

Decca 27356

Washington Square Dance (Ethel Merman with Chorus)
(Dance To The Music Of) The Ocarina (Gordon
   Jenkins Orchestra and Chorus)

Decca 27357

It's A Lovely Day Today (Dick Haymes and Eileen
   Wilson)

Once Upon A Time Today (Dick Haymes)

Decca 27358

Welcome To Lichtenburg (Gordon Jenkins Orchestra
    and Chorus)
They Like Ike (Gordon Jenkins Orchestra and
    Chorus)

Although nothing is so displeasing as the
"pleasing" singing of Dinah Shore (unless it's
Doris Day's), the 33-1/3 rpm 12" lp whereon she
attempted the Merman role, in that the original
supporting cast and (more importantly) the original arrangements were retained, merits the
designation "original cast album" a shade more
than the Decca. A further advantage was a 45
rpm extended-play disc, "Backstage At 'Call Me
Madam'" (engineered by Jeff Miller and Fred
Elsasser), given away by RCA Victor with each
purchase of a Dinah Shore "Call Me Madam" lp.
Amidst the background clatter of backstage
voices and onstage singing by everyone except
Miss Merman, Part 1 (CMM-1) featured Wayne
Howell interviewing Don Hershey, Sto Phelps,
Galina Talva, and a tittering Russell Nype;
Part 2 (CMM-2), an interview with Irving Berlin
himself.

Leland Hayward Presents
The Original Show Album of Irving Berlin's
CALL ME MADAM
With Dinah Shore and the Original Broadway Company

RCA Victor LOC-1000

_____

Side 1:

OVERTURE: (a) You're Just In Love; (b) The
Ocarina; (c) The Best Thing For You; (d) It's
A Lovely Day Today; (e) Something To Dance About

Mrs. Sally Adams (Chorus)
The Hostess With The Mostes' On The Ball (Dinah
    Shore)
Washington Square Dance (Dinah Shore)
Welcome To Lichtenburg (Paul Lucas)
Can You Use Any Money Today? (Dinah Shore)
Marrying For Love (Dinah Shore and Paul Lucas)
The Ocarina (Galina Talva)

Side 2:

It's A Lovely Day Today (Russell Nype and Galina
    Talva)
The Best Thing For You (Dinah Shore)   •
Something To Dance About (Dinah Shore)
Once Upon A Time Today (Russell Nype)
They Like Ike (Pat Harrington, Ralph Chambers, and
    Jay Velie)
(I Wonder Why) You're Just In Love (Dinah Shore
    and Russell Nype)

The four above-listed Russ Case recordings of
selections from "Call Me Madam" were reissued
on one side of 33-1/3 rpm 10" 1p MGM E-531,
c/w selections from Frank Loesser's "Guys And
Dolls". Another 33-1/3 rpm 10" 1p, Mercury MG-
25088, was likewise selections from "Call Me
Madam" c/w selections from "Guys And Dolls".
Four selections from "Call Me Madam" were released

on 45 rpm extended-play RCA Victor EOA-498, and could have been coupled on a 33-1/3 rpm 10" lp with the four selections from "Annie, Get Your Gun" that were released on 45 rpm extended-play RCA Victor ERA-4.

Earlier in 1950, MGM released the screen version of "Annie, Get Your Gun". Studio executives demonstrated their contempt for the public and what the public wanted by dismissing Judy Garland from the starring role after working her to death for years, then firing her for being unable to continue being worked. Judy got through some footage and recorded "They Say It's Wonderful" (with Howard Keel), "Anything You Can Do" (with Keel), "The Girl That I Marry" (imitating Keel, until she's required to break down), "Let's Go West Again" (with Chorus), "I Got The Sun In The Morning" (with Chorus), "I'm An Indian Too" (with Chorus), "Doin' What Comes Natur'lly" (with Children), "You Can't Get A Man With A Gun" (so far, Judy's only recording from this score that MGM has released to the record-buying public), "There's No Business Like Show Business" (with Howard Keel, Louis Calhern, and Keenan Wynn), and a solo recording of "Show Business", one chorus, but the one greatest recording, if I had to choose, that Judy ever made! All of these numbers, except "Let's Go West Again", were re-recorded by Betty Hutton, who replaced Judy Garland as well as Betty Hutton could, co-starring with Howard Keel and supported by Louis Calhern, Edward Arnold, J. Carrol Naish, Keenan Wynn, and Benay Venuta. Songs retained:

Anything You Can Do
Colonel Buffalo Bill
Doin' What Comes Natur'lly
The Girl That I Marry
I Got The Sun In The Morning
I'm An Indian Too
My Defenses Are Down
(There's No Business Like) Show Business
They Say It's Wonderful
You Can't Get A Man With A Gun

The following 33-1/3 rpm 10" sound-track lp was
also pressed on four 78 rpm discs comprising MGM
Album MGM-50. All eight selections are still
available on one side of 33-1/3 rpm 12" sound-
track lp MGM E3768, c/w songs from the sound-
track of the Bert Kalmar-Harry Ruby bio-pic "Three
Little Words" (originally 33-1/3 rpm 10" lp MGM
E-516).

Recorded Directly From The Sound Track
Of
The MGM Technicolor Musical

ANNIE GET YOUR GUN

Betty Hutton   Howard Keel

MGM E-509

Side 1:

I Got The Sun In The Morning (Betty Hutton)
They Say It's Wonderful (Betty Hutton and Howard
    Keel)
You Can't Get A Man With A Gun (Betty Hutton)

130

My Defenses Are Down (Howard Keel)

Side 2:

Doin' What Comes Natur'lly (Betty Hutton)
The Girl That I Marry (Howard Keel)
Anything You Can Do (Betty Hutton and Howard
  Keel)
(There's No Business Like) Show Business (Betty
  Hutton with Howard Keel, Louis Calhern, and
  Keenan Wynn)

1951:

With "Call Me Madam" wowing 'em on Broadway, and
"Annie, Get Your Gun" packing movie theatres all
over America, Berlin evidently figured it would
be bad business competing with himself. No new
Irving Berlin compositions were written or published this year.

1952:

Anthem For Presentation Theme
For The Very First Time
  Tony Martin, RCA Victor 20-4671 (78)
I Like Ike
  Campaign song for successful Presidential
  Candidate Dwight D. Eisenhower. This was a
  new lyric to Berlin's 1950 "They Like Ike",
  which had been, in fact, a pre-campaign song
  for the General. People turning on their TV
  sets, day or night, were likely to be confronted
  by Berlin, singing this song, plugging his
  candidate.

Promenade Band (vocal by Male Chorus), RCA
Victor 20-4578 (78)
Male Chorus (with Orchestra), Columbia CL-2260
(33-1/3)
Our Day Of Independence

<u>1953:</u>

Sittin' In The Sun (Countin' My Money)
    Berlin wrote this to be sung by Bing Crosby in
    the film "White Christmas". Due to innumerable
    delays in production, however, he decided to
    publish it independently.
    Louis Armstrong, Decca 28803 (78)
    Frankie Laine, Columbia 40036 (78)
What Does A Soldier Want For Christmas

<u>The film version of "Call Me Madam" featured Ethel
Merman, Donald O'Connor, George Sanders, and
Galina Talva, Miss Talva's songs being recorded,
for some unexplained reason, by Carole Richards.
Besides reviving "What Chance Have I With Love"
(originally from his 1940 show "Louisiana Purchase") for O'Connor, and his 1913 "The International Rag" for Miss Merman, Berlin wrote eight
bars of new lyrics for "Mrs. Sally Adams", sung
by a switchboard of gabbling telephone operators.
Only a few lines of "Welcome to Lichtenburg" were
sung (by a Chorus) in the background. Otherwise
numbers sung in film by same artists as in sound-
track album. Songs retained:</u>

The Best Thing For You
Can You Use Any Money Today?
The Hostess With The Mostes' On the Ball
The International Rag

132

It's A Lovely Day Today
Marrying For Love
Mrs. Sally Adams
(Dance To The Music Of) The Ocarina
Something To Dance About
Welcome To Lichtenburg
What Chance Have I With Love
(I Wonder Why) You're Just In Love

The following 33-1/3 rpm 10" sound-track lp was
also pressed on five 78 rpm discs comprising Decca
Album A-936 (Decca 28641 - 28645 inclusive) and in
45 rpm extended-play Decca Album ED-508 (Decca
91000 - 91001 inclusive).

A Decca Original Sound Track Album
From the 20th Century Fox
Technicolor Production Of

Irving Berlin's CALL ME MADAM

ETHEL MERMAN · DONALD O'CONNOR · GEORGE SANDERS

Decca DL-5465

Side 1:

The Hostess With The Mostes' On The Ball (Ethel
  Merman)
Can You Use Any Money Today? (Ethel Merman)
Marrying For Love (George Sanders)
It's A Lovely Day Today (Donald O'Connor and
  Carole Richards)
The International Rag (Ethel Merman)
(I Wonder Why) You're Just In Love (Ethel Merman

133

and Donald O'Connor)

Side 2:

(Dance To The Music Of) The Ocarina (Carole
   Richards)
What Chance Have I With Love (Donald O'Connor)
Something To Dance About (Donald O'Connor and
   Carole Richards)
The Best Thing For You (Ethel Merman and George
   Sanders)

FINALE: (a) You're Just In Love (Ethel Merman
   and George Sanders); (b) Something To Dance
   About (Chorus)

1954:

I'm Not Afraid (I Believe In America)
   Introduced on TV, April 9, 1954, by Eddie Fisher.
Is She The Only Girl In The World
I Still Like Ike
When It's Peach Blossom Time In Lichtenburg

The first of two 1954 Berlin filmusicals was
"White Christmas", featuring Bing Crosby, Danny
Kaye, Rosemary Clooney, Vera-Ellen, and Dean
Jagger. In addition to new numbers listed below
(actually written during 1953), Vera-Ellen did a
cute tap-dance to Berlin's "Abraham" (originally
from "Holiday Inn"); Crosby and Kaye sang a
Rhythm Montage of (a) "Heat Wave", (b) "Let Me
Sing And I'm Happy", (c) "Blue Skies"; and "Mandy"
was revived by all four musical stars (with
Ensemble) as a Minstrel Production Number. This
ballad has never been performed in any show or

film except as a Minstrel Production Number --
as, for example, by Eddie Cantor, George Murphy,
Ethel Merman, Ann Sothern (with Goldwyn Girls
including Lucille Ball) in 1934 film "Kid Millions"
-- except this time, to appease the history-
altering pressure-groups, it was sans blackface;
preceded by Crosby and Kaye singing "I Want To
See A Minstrel Show" (also from "Ziegfeld Follies
Of 1919") followed by Miss Clooney (as Interlocutor), Kaye and Crosby, singing a special
material routine of minstrel jokes set to music
(which may have been written by Berlin for any
production from "White Christmas" back to "Yip,
Yip, Yaphank"). Berlin score:

White Christmas
As first number in film, sung by Bing Crosby
during a World War II overseas show for weeping
G.I.s (they're weeping because they came to
the show expecting Jolson!); reprised as Finale
by Bing Crosby, Danny Kaye, Rosemary Clooney,
Vera-Ellen.
Bing Crosby, Danny Kaye, Peggy Lee, Trudy
Stevens (with Chorus), Decca 29342 (78)
The Best Things Happen While You're Dancing
Sung by Danny Kaye (with Chorus); danced by
Danny Kaye and Vera-Ellen.
Danny Kaye (with Skylarks), Decca 29290 (78)
Choreography
Sung and danced by Danny Kaye.
Danny Kaye (with Skylarks), Decca 29290 (78)
A Crooner - A Comic
During 1952, when this film was first conceived,
it was to have starred Bing Crosby and Fred
Astaire; for them, Berlin wrote this as "A
Singer - A Dancer" (as so written, Crosby
interpolating an excerpt from Berlin's "A

135

Pretty Girl Is Like A Melody"). During 1953, after Astaire got ill, "White Christmas" was to have starred Crosby and Donald O'Connor. During 1954, after O'Connor got ill and as finally released, it starred Crosby and Danny Kaye, for whom Berlin revised "A Singer - A Dancer" as "A Crooner - A Comic". After all this revision, the song was dropped and never used at all.

Count Your Blessings Instead Of Sheep
Sung by Bing Crosby; reprised (eight bars) by Crosby and Rosemary Clooney.
Bing Crosby, Decca 29251 (78)
Jimmy Durante, Warner Bros. W1506 (33-1/3)
Eddie Fisher (1954), RCA Victor 20-5871 (78)
Eddie Fisher (1965), Dot DLP-3648 (33-1/3)

Gee, I Wish I Was Back In The Army
Verse, first and third choruses, sung by Bing Crosby and Danny Kaye; second chorus sung by Rosemary Clooney and Vera-Ellen. Third chorus contains a reference to Al Jolson, callously omitted by Crosby and Kaye on the following recording.
Bing Crosby and Danny Kaye (medley), Decca 29341 (78)

The Old Man
Sung twice by Male Chorus.
Bing Crosby and Danny Kaye (medley), Decca 29341 (78)

Love, You Didn't Do Right By Me
Sung by Rosemary Clooney.
Dorsey Brothers Orchestra (vocal by Bill Raymond), Bell 1073 (78)
Peggy Lee, Decca 29250 (78)

Sisters
Sung by Rosemary Clooney and Vera-Ellen; later

136

lip-synched by Kaye and Crosby.
Tommy and Jimmy Dorsey (vocal: "Brothers") and
their Orchestra, Bell 1073 (78)
Peggy Lee (singing a duet with herself), Decca
29250 (78)

Snow
Sung by Bing Crosby, Danny Kaye, Rosemary
Clooney, Vera-Ellen. This was a new lyric to
the molody of Berlin's 1955 "Free".
Bing Crosby, Danny Kaye, Peggy Lee, Trudy
Stevens (with Chorus), Decca 29342 (78)

What Can You Do With A General
Sung by Bing Crosby
Bing Crosby, Decca 29251 (78)

.

The following 33-1/3 rpm 12" original cast lp was
also pressed in 78 rpm, Decca Album A-956 (Decca
29251, 29290, 29250, 29341 ["Blue Skies" deleted],
29342) and in 45 rpm extended-play, Decca Album
ED-819 (Decca 91463 - 91465 inclusive).

Selections From Irving Berlin's

WHITE CHRISTMAS

A Paramount Production In VistaVision

BING CROSBY · DANNY KAYE · And PEGGY LEE

Decca DL-8083

Side 1:

MEDLEY: (a) The Old Man; (b) Gee, I Wish I Was
Back In The Army (Bing Crosby and Danny Kaye)

137

Sisters (Peggy Lee)
The Best Things Happen While You're Dancing
   (Danny Kaye with Skylarks)
Snow (Bing Crosby, Danny Kaye, Peggy Lee, Trudy
   Stevens)

MEDLEY: (a) Blue Skies; (b) I Want To See A
   Minstrel Show; (c) Mandy (Bing Crosby and Danny
   Kaye with Chorus)

Side 2:

Choreography (Danny Kaye with Skylarks)
Count Your Blessings Instead Of Sheep (Bing
   Crosby)
Love, You Didn't Do Right By Me (Peggy Lee)
What Can You Do With A General (Bing Crosby)
White Christmas (Bing Crosby, Danny Kaye, Peggy
   Lee, Trudy Stevens)

Well after the release of Rosemary Clooney's
"Love, You Didn't Do Right By Me" c/w "Sisters"
as a single, Columbia decided to issue the
following 33-1/3 rpm 10" original cast lp of
their own. Side 1 was also pressed in 45 rpm
extended-play on Columbia B-1900; Side 2 also
pressed in 45 rpm extended-play on Columbia
B-1901.

ROSEMARY CLOONEY
In Songs From The Paramount Pictures
Production of

Irving Berlin's WHITE CHRISTMAS

Side 1:

White Christmas
Mandy
Snow
Gee, I Wish I Was Back In The Army

Side 2:

Love, You Didn't Do Right By Me
Sisters (with Betty Clooney)
The Best Things Happen While You're Dancing
Count Your Blessings Instead Of Sheep

Berlin's second 1954 filmusical was "There's No
Business Like Show Business", with Ethel Merman,
Donald O'Connor, Marilyn Monroe, Dan Dailey,
Johnnie Ray, and Mitzi Gaynor. In addition to
new numbers listed below, "Alexander's Ragtime
Band" was presented early in the film as one of
the largest, lushest, and most foolish production
numbers of all time, sung by Ethel Merman and
Dan Dailey in German dialect, Donald O'Connor in
Scotch dialect, Mitzi Gaynor in French dialect,
and Johnnie Ray in pseudo-blues style, all of
whom were joined by Marilyn Monroe and several
million other people to reprise this and "There's
No Business Like Show Business" as the Finale.
Other Berlin standards, and those who sang them,
included: "After You Get What You Want, You
Don't Want It" (Marilyn Monroe), "Heat Wave"
(Marilyn Monroe), "If You Believe" (Johnnie Ray),

"Lazy" (Marilyn Monroe), "Let's Have Another Cup
O'Coffee" (excerpt sung by Ethel Merman), "A Man
Chases A Girl (Until She Catches Him)" (sung and
danced by Donald O'Connor), "Play A Simple Melody"
(Ethel Merman and Dan Dailey), "A Pretty Girl Is
Like A Melody" (Ethel Merman and Dan Dailey),
"There's No Business Like Show Business" (Ethel
Merman), "When The Midnight Choo-Choo Leaves For
Alabam'" (sung by Ethel Merman and Dan Dailey;
reprised by Mitzi Gaynor and Donald O'Connor),
"You'd Be Surprised" (excerpt sung by Dan Dailey).
Additional Berlin oldies were played ("Call Me Up
Some Rainy Afternoon"; others) or sung ("Marie";
"Remember") as incidental background. For this
film Berlin wrote only the following three new
selections:

But I Ain't Got A Man
    Sung by Marilyn Monroe. This was withdrawn from
    the film before release, possibly due to anti-
    sexiness censorship of the sort that forced
    Miss Monroe's "After You Get What You Want You
    Don't Want It" to be cut from all showings in
    Canada.
I Can Make You Laugh (But I Wish I Could Make You
Cry)
    Sung by Donald O'Connor. This also was with-
    drawn from the film before release.
    Eddie Fisher made an RCA Victor recording of
    this song which wasn't released either.
A Sailor's Not A Sailor ('Til A Sailor's Been
Tattooed)
    Sung by Ethel Merman and Mitzi Gaynor. This
    would up the only new song in the film.
    Ethel Merman and Mitzi Gaynor, Decca 90059
    (12") (78)

140

Now RCA Victor revenged themselves upon Decca for the Ethel Merman deal of several years back. Decca obtained exclusive rights to release the sound-track lp, but commercial sales of all sound-track vocals by Marilyn Monroe then belonged to RCA Victor. In an otherwise authentic album, Decca was forced to record Dolores Gray in carbon-copy vocals of Miss Monroe's numbers. The following 33-1/3 rpm 12" sound-track lp was also pressed on three 78 rpm twelve-inch discs (Decca 90057, 90058, 90059) and in 45 rpm extended-play, Decca Album ED-828 (Decca 91485 - 91487 inclusive).

Selections From The Sound Track
Of
Darryl F. Zanuck's Presentation Of
Irving Berlin's

THERE'S NO BUSINESS LIKE SHOW BUSINESS

A 20th Century Fox Production
In CinemaScope

ETHEL MERMAN · DONALD O'CONNOR · DAN DAILEY ·
JOHNNIE RAY · MITZI GAYNOR · And DOLORES GRAY

With the 20th Century Fox
Orchestra And Chorus
Ken Darby, Vocal Director
Alfred Newman And Lionel Newman, Musical Directors

Decca DL-8091

Side 1:

There's No Business Like Show Business (Ethel Merman)

141

When The Midnight Choo-Choo Leaves For Alabam'
(Ethel Merman and Dan Dailey)
Play A Simple Melody (Ethel Merman and Dan
Dailey)
After You Get What You Want You Don't Want It
(Dolores Gray)
If You Believe (Johnnie Ray)
A Man Chases A Girl (Until She Catches Him)
(Donald O'Connor)
Lazy (Dolores Gray)

Side 2:

Heat Wave (Dolores Gray)
A Sailor's Not A Sailor ('Til A Sailor's Been
Tattooed) (Ethel Merman and Mitzi Gaynor)
Alexander's Ragtime Band (Ethel Merman, Dan
Dailey, Donald O'Connor, Mitzi Gaynor, Johnnie
Ray)

FINALE: (a) Alexander's Ragtime Band; (b) There
No Business Like Show Business (Ensemble)

And RCA Victor released the following 45 rpm
extended-play disc of Marilyn Monroe's vocals fr
the sound-track. Two of these, "Heat Wave" and
"After You Get What You Want You Don't Want It",
were also issued on 45 rpm single RCA Victor 47-
6033. These and a third, "Lazy", were re-releas
following Marilyn's death, along with sound-
track vocals from several of her other films, on
33-1/3 rpm 12" lp 20th Fox FXG-5000. The fourth
"You'd Be Surprised", is a real collector's item
having been recorded for "There's No Business
Like Show Business", but not used therein.

142

MARILYN MONROE
In
Irving Berlin's

THERE'S NO BUSINESS LIKE SHOW BUSINESS

RCA Victor EPA-593

Side 1:

You'd Be Surprised
Heat Wave

Side 2:

Lazy
After You Get What You Want You Don't Want It

1955:

Aesop, That Able Fable Man
The Most
Out Of This World Into My Arms
Please Let Me Come Back To You

1956:

Anybody Can Write
Ike For Four More Years
　　(melody based on nursery rhyme "Three Blind Mice")
　　Campaign song for successful second-term Presi-
　　dential Candidate Dwight D. Eisenhower. Intro-
　　duced by Irving Berlin at 1956 Republican National
　　Convention.

143

I Never Want To See You Again
It Takes More Than Love To Keep A Lady Warm
Klondike Kate
Love Leads To Marriage
Opening The Mizner Story
Smiling Geisha
When A One Star General's Daughter Meets A Four
    Star General's Son
You're A Sentimental Guy
You're A Sucker For A Dame

1957:

(You Can't Lose The Blues With) Colors
    Rosemary Clooney, Columbia 4-40981 (45)
I Keep Running Away From You
    Don Cherry, Columbia 4-41014 (45)
I'll Know Better The Next Time
Irving Berlin Barrett
Sayonara
    Theme-Song of Marlon Brando film "Sayonara".
    This was a previously unpublished number,
    actually written during 1953 under the title
    "Sayonara, Sayonara".
    Eddie Fisher, RCA Victor 47-7051 (45)
Silver Platter
Song For Elizabeth Esther Barrett
When Love Was All

During the final months of 1957, Mary Martin, wh
had been touring Summer Stock in "Annie, Get
Your Gun", brought her version to TV for an NBC
Special. The same songs were sung thereon, and
by the same artists, as on the following 33-1/3
rpm 12" tie-in lp.

144

"ANNIE GET YOUR GUN"

Mary Martin · John Raitt

Capitol W-913

Side 1:

OVERTURE: (a) I Got The Sun In The Morning; (b)
  Show Business; (c) They Say It's Wonderful; (d)
  The Girl That I Marry; (e) They Say It's Wonder-
  ful

I'm A Bad, Bad Man (John Raitt)
Doin' What Comes Natur'lly (Mary Martin)
The Girl That I Marry (John Raitt)
You Can't Get A Man With A Gun (Mary Martin)
Moonshine Lullaby (Mary Martin)
They Say It's Wonderful (Mary Martin and John
  Raitt)

Side 2:

My Defenses Are Down (John Raitt)
I'm An Indian Too (Mary Martin)
I Got Lost In His Arms (Mary Martin)
I Got The Sun In The Morning (Mary Martin)
Anything You Can Do (Mary Martin and John Raitt)

FINALE: (a) There's No Business Like Show
  Business; (b) They Say It's Wonderful (Mary
  Martin and John Raitt)

1958:

145

According to the Library Of Congress Copyright
Records, Berlin appears to have written nothing
this year. One wonders if most songs he's
written since 1954 have been published.

1959:

Israel

1960: 1961:

Sam, Sam (The Man What Am)
This song was copyrighted both years; probably
the second is a revision of the first.

1962:

If You Haven't Got An Ear For Music
Poor Joe
The Popular Song
Who Would Have Thought

On October 20, 1962, opened Berlin's latest
Broadway show: "Mr. President". In the cast
were Robert Ryan, Nanette Fabray, Anita Gillette
Jack Haskell, Jack Washburn, Stanley Grover,
Jerry Strickler, Charlotte Fairchild, Wisa
D'Orso, and David Brooks. Berlin score:

Don't Be Afraid Of Romance
Sung by Jack Washburn.
Empty Pockets Filled With Love
Sung as a counter-melody duet by Jack Haskell
and Anita Gillette. In an earlier draft, this
number was first called "Empty Pockets (But A
Heart Full Of Love)".

146

The First Lady
   Sung by Nanette Fabray.
Glad To Be Home
   Sung by Nanette Fabray and Ensemble. This was
   a new lyric to the melody of Berlin's 1957
   "I Keep Running Away From You".
I'm Gonna Get Him
   Sung by Nanette Fabray and Anita Gillette. This
   was a previously unpublished number, actually
   written during 1956.
   Vicki Belmonte, Cadence 1430 (45)
In Our Hide-Away
   Sung by Nanette Fabray and Robert Ryan.
Is He The Only Man In The World
   Sung by Nanette Fabray and Anita Gillette.
   This was a rewrite of Berlin's 1954 "Is She
   The Only Girl In The World".
It Gets Lonely In The White House
   Sung by Robert Ryan.
I've Got To Be Around
   Sung by Jack Haskell.
Laugh It Up
   Sung by Nanette Fabray, Robert Ryan, Anita
   Gillette, Jerry Strickler.
Let's Go Back To The Waltz
   Sung by Nanette Fabray and Ensemble.
Meat And Potatoes
   Sung by Jack Haskell and Stanley Grover.
Mr. President
   Withdrawn from show.
Once Ev'ry Four Years
   Withdrawn from show.
The Only Dance I Know
   Sung by Wisa D'Orso and Girls. This was a
   vocal version of "Song For Belly Dancer".
Opening

Sung by David Brooks. This number introduced
"Mr. President", explaining that the pro-
tagonist wasn't a take-off on Roosevelt, Truma
Eisenhower, Kennedy, or any other individual,
but just a spoof on the United States Preside
in general.
Pigtails And Freckles
Sung by Jack Haskell and Anita Gillette.
The Secret Service
Sung by Anita Gillette, the only member of th
cast who could carry a tune.
Vicki Belmonte, Cadence 1430 (45)
Song For Belly Dancer
Played by Jay Blackton Orchestra. This was a
instrumental version of "The Only Dance I Kno
They Love Me
Sung by Nanette Fabray.
This Is A Great Country
Finale - sung by Robert Ryan with Entire Comp
Bing Crosby, Reprise F-2020 (33-1/3)
The Washington Twist
Sung by Anita Gillette and Dancers.
You Need A Hobby
Sung by Nanette Fabray and Robert Ryan.

At least two 33-1/3 rpm 12" lp's were released
of songs from this show: one by Perry Como and
Company (RCA Victor), since deleted, and the
following original cast album.

Leland Hayward Presents
ROBERT RYAN · NANETTE FABRAY
In

MR. PRESIDENT

Music and Lyrics by IRVING BERLIN

Columbia KOL-5870

Side 1:

Opening (David Brooks)
Let's Go Back To The Waltz (Nanette Fabray and
  Chorus)
In Our Hide-Away (Robert Ryan and Nanette Fabray)
The First Lady (Nanette Fabray)
Meat And Potatoes (Jack Haskell and Stanley
  Grover)
I've Got To Be Around (Jack Haskell)
The Secret Service (Anita Gillette)
It Gets Lonely In The White House (Robert Ryan)
Is He The Only Man In The World (Anita Gillette
  and Nanette Fabray)
They Love Me (Nanette Fabray and Chorus)

Side 2:

Pigtails And Freckles (Anita Gillette and Jack
  Haskell)
Don't Be Afraid Of Romance (Jack Washburn)
Laugh It Up (Anita Gillette, Jerry Strickler,
  Robert Ryan, Nanette Fabray)
Empty Pockets Filled With Love (Anita Gillette
  and Jack Haskell)
Glad To Be Home (Nanette Fabray and Chorus)
You Need A Hobby (Robert Ryan and Nanette Fabray)
The Washington Twist (Anita Gillette)
The Only Dance I Know (Wisa D'Orso and Girls)
I'm Gonna Get Him (Anita Gillette and Nanette
  Fabray)

149

This Is A Great Country (Robert Ryan and Company

1963:

(It's) Always The Same
A Guy On Monday
A Man To Cook For
One Man Woman
Outside Of Loving You, I Like You
The P.X.
The Ten Best Undressed Women
Whisper It

1964:

Let Me Sing

1965:

I Used To Play It By Ear

1966:

An Old Fashioned Wedding
    Interpolated in Lincoln Center revival of
    "Annie, Get Your Gun"
(Who Needs) The Birds And The Bees
Long As I Can Take You Home
Wait Until You're Married

As one in a series of musical comedy revivals at
the Music Theatre of Lincoln Center, N.Y., Presi
dent and Producing Director Richard Rodgers re-
presented the 20-year-old "Annie, Get Your Gun"
with the original star, Ethel Merman. The same
numbers were sung therein, and by the same

artists, as on the following 33-1/3 rpm 12"
original cast lp.

An Original Cast Album

ETHEL MERMAN
In
ANNIE GET YOUR GUN

Music & Lyrics By Irving Berlin

RCA Victor LOC-1124

Side 1:

OVERTURE: (a) I Got The Sun In The Morning;
(b) Show Business; (c) They Say It's Wonderful;
(d) You Can't Get A Man With A Gun; (e) The Girl
That I Marry; (f) I'm An Indian Too; (g) They Say
It's Wonderful

Colonel Buffalo Bill (Jerry Orbach, Benay
   Venuta, and Ensemble)
I'm A Bad, Bad Man (Bruce Yarnell and Girls)
Doin' What Comes Natur'lly (Ethel Merman, Ronn
   Carroll, and Children)
The Girl That I Marry (Bruce Yarnell)
You Can't Get A Man With A Gun (Ethel Merman)
(There's No Business Like) Show Business (Ethel
   Merman, Bruce Yarnell, Rufus Smith, Jerry
   Orbach)
They Say It's Wonderful (Ethel Merman and Bruce
   Yarnell)

Moonshine Lullaby (Ethel Merman, Trio and
   Children)
(There's No Business Like) Show Business (Ethel
   Merman)
My Defenses Are Down (Bruce Yarnell and Boys)
I'm An Indian Too (Ethel Merman)
I Got Lost In His Arms (Ethel Merman and Singers)
I Got The Sun In The Morning (Ethel Merman and
   Company)
An Old Fashioned Wedding (counter-melody duet by
   Ethel Merman and Bruce Yarnell)
Anything You Can Do (Ethel Merman and Bruce
   Yarnell)

FINALE: (a) (There's No Business Like) Show
   Business; (b) They Say It's Wonderful (Entire
   Company)

In addition to previously listed original cast
and sound-track albums of Irving Berlin shows
and film scores, single recordings of individual
songs, etc., other album collections of Berlin
songs have been released which will be itemized
directly below. During the 1930's, these
included two 78 rpm albums by Paul Whiteman and
his Orchestra (vocals by Clark Dennis and Joan
Edwards), each consisting of five ten-inch discs:
"Irving Berlin Songs, Volume 1", Decca A-70
(Decca 2690 - 2694 inclusive); "Irving Berlin
Songs, Volume 2", Decca A-71 (Decca 2695 -
2699 inclusive). Volume 1 contained "Say It With
Music", "Lady Of The Evening", "All Alone",
"Remember", "How Deep Is The Ocean", "Russian
Lullaby", "Crinoline Days", "Tell Me, Little Gypsy",

and two others; contents of Volume 2 unknown. Additionally, four of the previously noted recordings by Frank Sinatra were reissued to comprise a 45 rpm extended-play disc, "Frank Sinatra Sings Irving Berlin", Columbia B-1524; contents again unknown. The following 45 rpm single is also of interest.

Frankie Carle (piano),
RCA Victor 47-4091

MEDLEY: (a) Marie; (b) Cheek To Cheek

MEDLEY: (a) How Deep Is The Ocean?; (b) When I Lost You; (c) Nobody Knows (And Nobody Seems To Care)

The following 33-1/3 rpm long-playing records are all ten-inch. Additional 10" lp's include "Irving Berlin, All Time Hits" (Royale 6016), "Irving Berlin, A Symphonic Portrait" (Capitol L276), and "Irving Berlin Waltzes" (MGM E-216), the latter by Paul Britten, also released in 45 rpm extended-play on MGM X-1034 (Volume 1) and MGM X-1035 (Volume 2). Contents of these three lp's, being unknown, are for that reason not itemized.

Following album also pressed in 78 rpm, Decca A-656 (Decca 24224 - 24226 inclusive) and the single (Decca 24660) of selections from "Miss Liberty".

ANDREWS SISTERS

IRVING BERLIN SONGS

153

Side 1:

Alexander's Ragtime Band
I Want To Go Back To Michigan
Heat Wave
When The Midnight Choo-Choo Leaves For Alabam'

Side 2:

Some Sunny Day
How Many Times?
Homework (from "Miss Liberty")
Only For Americans (from "Miss Liberty")

Following album: Side 1 also pressed in 45 rpm
extended-play on RCA Victor EPA-488; Side 2 also
pressed in 45 rpm extended-play on RCA Victor
EPA-426.

Eddie Fisher Sings
Irving Berlin Favorites

RCA Victor LPM-3122

Side 1:

With You (from "Puttin' On The Ritz")
How About Me?
How Deep Is The Ocean?
When I Leave The World Behind

Side 2:

Cheek To Cheek
They Say It's Wonderful
All By Myself
Remember

<u>Following album also pressed in 78 rpm, Columbia</u>
<u>C-78 (Columbia 36449-36452 inclusive).</u>

Al Goodman And His Orchestra
THE MUSIC OF IRVING BERLIN

Columbia CL-6041

Side 1:

Alexander's Ragtime Band
Say It With Music
Blue Skies
All Alone

Side 2:

Lady Of The Evening
Remember
Say It Isn't So
Always

<u>Following album also pressed in 78 rpm, Decca A-</u>
<u>654 (Decca 24420 - 24423 inclusive).</u>

Dick Haymes Sings
Carmen Cavallaro At The Piano
Irving Berlin Songs

Decca DL-5023

Side 1:

Say It With Music
The Song Is Ended
Cheek To Cheek
Say It Isn't So

Side 2:

Soft Lights And Sweet Music
The Girl On The Magazine Cover
All Alone
Lady Of The Evening

<u>Following album also pressed in 78 rpm (RCA Victor
P-266), 45 rpm standard-play (RCA Victor WP-266),
and 45 rpm extended-play (RCA Victor EPA-266).</u>

Sammy Kaye Plays Irving Berlin

RCA Victor LPM-15

Side 1:

A Pretty Girl Is Like A Melody
Alexander's Ragtime Band
Always

Side 2:

Blue Skies
How Deep Is The Ocean?
Say It Isn't So

156

Following album also pressed in 78 rpm, RCA Victor P-159 (RCA Victor 20-1896 - 20-1899 inclusive), 45 rpm standard-play, RCA Victor WP-159 (RCA Victor 47-2780 - 47-2783 inclusive), and 45 rpm extended-play two-record set, RCA Victor EPB-3057. Vocal choruses by Earl Randall and Nancy Evans.

THE SONGS OF IRVING BERLIN
Wayne King and his Orchestra

RCA Victor LPM-3057

Side 1:

Always
Blue Skies
All Alone
Say It With Music

Side 2:

Remember
A Pretty Girl Is Like A Melody
What'll I Do
Alexander's Ragtime Band

Following album also pressed in 45 rpm standard-play, Columbia B-307.

Lee Wiley Sings Irving Berlin

Columbia CL-6216

How Deep Is The Ocean?
Some Sunny Day
I Got Lost In His Arms
Heat Wave

Side 2:

Soft Lights And Sweet Music
Fools Fall In Love
How Many Times?
Supper Time?

Following album also pressed in 78 rpm, Decca
27107 - 27110 inclusive.

THE MUSIC OF IRVING BERLIN
Peter Yorke and his Concert Orchestra

Decca DL-5269

Side 1:

A Pretty Girl Is Like A Melody
Marie
I've Got My Love To Keep Me Warm
They Say It's Wonderful

Side 2:

The Song Is Ended
Cheek To Cheek
The Girl That I Marry
Lady Of The Evening

<u>Following album also pressed in 78 rpm, Decca</u>
<u>27287 - 27290 inclusive.</u>

SAY IT WITH MUSIC
Irving Berlin Compositions
Victor Young and his Singing Strings

Decca DL-5294

Side 1:

Say It With Music
All Alone
Always
What'll I Do

Side 2:

Remember
Say It Isn't So
How Deep Is The Ocean?
Soft Lights And Sweet Music

<u>The following 33-1/3 rpm long-playing records</u>
<u>are all twelve-inch. Additional 12" lp's include</u>
<u>"Irving Berlin Songs" (Mercury MG-20813) and "The</u>
<u>Best of Berlin" (Mercury MG-20316), the latter</u>
<u>by Sarah Vaughan and Billy Eckstine. Contents</u>
<u>of these lp's, being unknown, are for that reason</u>
<u>not listed, although Eckstine and Miss Vaughn</u>
<u>sing "Alexander's Ragtime Band" and eleven ballads,</u>
<u>none of which they're equipped to handle.</u>

LET ME SING AND I'M HAPPY
(The Best Of Irving Berlin)

Side 1:

MEDLEY: (a) Easter Parade; (b) White Christmas

RAGTIME MEDLEY: (a) Everybody's Doing It Now;
(b) Mandy; (c) Snookey Ookums; (d) Marie From
Sunny Italy; (e) The Ragtime Violin; (f) Alexander's Ragtime Band

MEDLEY: (a) A Pretty Girl Is Like A Melody; (b)
Say It With Music

MEDLEY: (a) Not For All The Rice In China; (b)
I'll See You In C-U-B-A; (c) I Want To Go Back
To Michigan

MEDLEY: (a) Russian Lullaby; (b) What'll I Do;
(c) The Song Is Ended

"BLUE SKIES" MEDLEY: (a) Puttin' On The Ritz;
(b) You Keep Coming Back Like A Song; (c) All
By Myself; (d) Blue Skies

Side 2:

MEDLEY: (a) Say It Isn't So; (b) How Deep Is Th
Ocean?

"TOP HAT" MEDLEY: (a) Top Hat, White Tie, And
Tails; (b) The Piccolino; (c) Isn't This A

Lovely Day?; (d) Cheek To Cheek

MEDLEY: (a) Remember; (b) All Alone; (c) Always

MEDLEY: (a) Let Me Sing And I'm Happy; (b) Play A Simple Melody

BITS OF THE BEST OF BERLIN (excerpts)

(a) Say It With Music; (b) Alexander's Ragtime Band; (c) Everybody Step; (d) Call Me Up Some Rainy Afternoon; (e) Everybody's Doing It Now; (f) When The Midnight Choo-Choo Leaves For Alabam'; (g) Snookey Ookums; (h) I'll See You In C-U-B-A; (i) I Want To Go Back To Michigan; (j) All By Myself; (k) Crinoline Days; (1) Oh! How I Hate To Get Up In The Morning; (m) Blue Skies; (n) Marie; (o) Let Yourself Go; (p) Soft Lights And Sweet Music; (q) Heat Wave; (r) Let's Have Another Cup O' Coffee; (s) Say It Isn't So; (t) Cheek To Cheek; (u) Isn't This A Lovely Day?; (v) The Piccolino; (w) Top Hat, White Tie, And Tails; (x) I'm Putting All My Eggs In One Basket; (y) Let's Face The Music And Dance; (z) Steppin' Out With My Baby; (a') Slumming On Park Avenue; (b') Easter Parade; (c') White Christmas; (d') This Is The Army, Mister Jones; (e') I'm Getting Tired So I Can Sleep; (f') I Left My Heart At The Stage Door Canteen; (g') American Eagles; (h') How About A Cheer For The Navy?; (i') Play A Simple Melody; (j') Anything You Can Do; (k') Doin' What Comes Natur'lly; (1') I Got The Sun In The Morning; (m') There's No Business Like Show Business; (n') You're Just In Love; (o') Count Your Blessings Instead Of Sheep; (p') Give Me Your

Tired, Your Poor; (q') God Bless America

Following album also pressed in 45 rpm extended-
play three-record set, Decca ED-811 (Decca 91304 -
91306 inclusive). Selections marked with an
asterick (*) accompanied by Ann Stockton at the
harp.

REMEMBER, The Waltzes Of Irving Berlin
Jesse Crawford, The Poet Of The Organ

Decca DL-8071

Side 1:

Remember *
The Song Is Ended
Always *
Marie
Because I Love You *
To Be Forgotten

Side 2:

All Alone *
Reaching For The Moon
What'll I Do *
The Girl That I Marry
Where Is The Song Of Songs For Me?
What Does It Matter? *

Following two MGM albums are comprised of previously
issued recordings.

THE VERY BEST OF IRVING BERLIN

Side 1:

(There's No Business Like) Show Business (Betty Hutton with Howard Keel, Louis Calhern, and Keenan Wynn)
Top Hat, White Tie, And Tails (Louis Armstrong)
Be Careful, It's My Heart (Russ Morgan)
You're Just In Love (Dancing Voices)
Better Luck Next Time (Judy Garland)
You Can't Get A Man With A Gun (Judy Garland)

Side 2:

Alexander's Ragtime Band (Irene Reid)
Cheek To Cheek (Bing Crosby)
The Girl That I Marry (Howard Keel)
It Only Happens When I Dance With You (Fred Astaire)
I Got The Sun In The Morning (Artie Shaw and his Orchestra)
God Bless America (Kate Smith)

Recorded Directly From The Sound Track
Of
The MGM Technicolor Musicals

ANNIE GET YOUR GUN

EASTER PARADE

MGM E3227

Side 1:

They Say It's Wonderful (Betty Hutton and Howard
Keel)
You Can't Get A Man With A Gun (Betty Hutton)
Doin' What Comes Natur'lly (Betty Hutton)
The Girl That I Marry (Howard Keel)
Anything You Can Do (Betty Hutton and Howard
Keel)
(There's No Business Like) Show Business (Betty
Hutton with Howard Keel, Louis Calhern, and
Keenan Wynn)

Side 2:

Easter Parade (Judy Garland and Fred Astaire
with Chorus)
A Couple Of Swells (Judy Garland and Fred Astaire)
Steppin' Out With My Baby (Fred Astaire)
A Fella With An Umbrella (Judy Garland and Peter
Lawford)

MEDLEY: (a) I Love A Piano (Judy Garland); (b)
Snookey Ookums (Judy Garland and Fred Astaire);
(c) When The Midnight Choo-Choo Leaves For
Alabam' (Judy Garland and Fred Astaire)

Shaking The Blues Away (Ann Miller)

Ella Fitzgerald Sings
THE IRVING BERLIN SONG BOOK

Arrangements and Orchestra Conducted by Paul Weston
Verve MGV-4019-2

164

Side 1:

Let's Face The Music And Dance
You're Laughing At Me
Let Yourself Go
You Can Have Him
Russian Lullaby
Puttin' On The Ritz
Get Thee Behind Me, Satan
Alexander's Ragtime Band

Side 2:

Top Hat, White Tie, And Tails
How About Me?
Cheek To Cheek
I Used To Be Color Blind
Lazy
How Deep Is The Ocean?
All By Myself
Remember

Side 3:

Supper Time
How's Chances
Heat Wave
Isn't This A Lovely Day?
You Keep Coming Back Like A Song
Reaching For The Moon
Slumming On Park Avenue

Side 4:

The Song Is Ended
I'm Putting All My Eggs In One Basket

Now It Can Be Told
Always
It's A Lovely Day Today
Change Partners
No Strings (I'm Fancy Free)
I've Got My Love To Keep Me Warm

BURL IVES SINGS IRVING BERLIN

United Artists UAL-3117

Side 1:

Alexander's Ragtime Band
Let's Have Another Cup O' Coffee
Say It Isn't So
I Love A Piano
What'll I Do
The International Rag

Side 2:

Everybody's Doing It Now
All Alone
I Want To Go Back To Michigan
Always
You'd Be Surprised
At The Devil's Ball

Ben Bagley's
IRVING BERLIN REVISITED

MGM SE-4435-OC

Beautiful Faces (Need Beautiful Clothes) (Dorothy
  Loudon, Bobby Short, William H. Elliott, Miles
  Kreuger)
Lonely Heart (Richard Chamberlain)
It'll Come To You (Blossom Dearie and Bobby Short)
Mr. Monotony (Dorothy Loudon)
Fools Fall In Love (Richard Chamberlain)

MEDLEY: (a) Back To Back; (b) The Yam (Dorothy
  Loudon and Bobby Short)

Side 2:

Louisiana Purchase (Dorothy Loudon, Bobby Short,
  William H. Elliott)
How's Chances (Richard Chamberlain)
Harlem On My Mind (Bobby Short)
Wild About You (Blossom Dearie)
Waiting At The End Of The Road (Dorothy Loudon
  and Bobby Short)
I'm Getting Tired So I Can Sleep (Richard
  Chamberlain)
I'd Rather Lead A Band (Bobby Short, Dorothy
  Loudon, Blossom Dearie)

IRVING BERLIN · ALL BY MYSELF
Volume 1
Everybody Step · 1921-1926
Monmouth Evergreen MES/6809

Side 1:

167

All By Myself (Steve Clayton)
Everybody Step (Annette Sanders)
Say It With Music (Jack Manno Singers)
Some Sunny Day (Rusty Dedrick Orchestra)
Crinoline Days (Steve Clayton)
Pack Up Your Sins And Go To The Devil (Annette
   Sanders)
Lady Of The Evening (Jack Manno Singers)
An Orange Grove In California (Steve Clayton)

Side 2:

MEDLEY: (a) All Alone (Annette Sanders); (b)
   What'll I Do? (Steve Clayton)
Tell Her In The Springtime (Jack Manno Singers)
Lazy (Annette Sanders)
Always (Steve Clayton)
Remember (Annette Sanders)
How Many Times (Jack Manno Singers)

IRVING BERLIN · ALL BY MYSELF
Volume 2
Puttin' On The Ritz · 1926-1930
Monmouth Evergreen MES/6810

Side 1:

We'll Never Know (Annette Sanders)
Russian Lullaby (Steve Clayton)
Together, We Two (Rusty Dedrick Orchestra)
Blue Skies (Annette Sanders)

MEDLEY: (a) It All Belongs To Me (Steve Clayton)
   (b) It's Up To The Band (Annette Sanders); (c)

168

Rainbow Of Girls (Jack Manno Singers); (d)
Shaking The Blues Away (Annette Sanders)

The Song Is Ended (Jack Manno Singers)

Side 2:

Let Me Sing And I'm Happy (Steve Clayton)
Roses Of Yesterday (Jack Manno Singers)
How About Me (Annette Sanders)

MEDLEY: (a) Marie; (b) Coquette (Jack Manno
  Singers

With You (Steve Clayton)
Puttin' On The Ritz (Rusty Dedrick Orchestra)
Reaching For The Moon (Annette Sanders)
Waiting At The End Of The Road (Jack Manno Singers)

IRVING BERLIN · ALL BY MYSELF
Volume 3
Heat Wave · 1930-1933
Monmouth Evergreen MES/6811

Side 1:

Little Things In Life (Rusty Dedrick Orchestra)
Begging For Love (Steve Clayton)
I Say It's Spinach (Jack Manno Singers)

MEDLEY: (a) Let's Have Another Cup O' Coffee
  (Annette Sanders); (b) On A Roof In Manhattan
  (Steve Clayton); (c) Soft Lights And Sweet
  Music (Jack Manno Singers)

169

MEDLEY: (a) How Deep Is The Ocean? (Annette Sanders); (b) Say It Isn't So (Steve Clayton)

I Can't Remember (Steve Clayton and Jack Manno Singers)
I'm Playing With Fire (Annette Sanders)

Side 2:

Maybe I Love You Too Much (Steve Clayton)
Harlem On My Mind (Rusty Dedrick Orchestra)
Not For All The Rice In China (Jack Manno Singers)
How's Chances (Steve Clayton)
Heat Wave (Jack Manno Singers)
Supper Time (Annette Sanders)
Easter Parade (Jack Manno Singers)

Irving Berlin Songography

CORRECTIONS and ADDENDA:

Irving Berlin's "We'll Never Know" was written and published during 1926, <u>not</u> 1938.

LETTER FROM IRVING BERLIN TO GROUCHO MARX, April 23, 1956: "... there are some songs I would be tempted to pay you not to do. For instance, "Cohen Owes Me $97" would not be taken in the same spirit it was taken when I wrote it for Belle Baker when she opened at the Palace many, many years ago. "The Friars Parade" is a bad special song I wrote for the Friars Club and you certainly would never have occasion to use that."

Melody of the song "I Lost My Shirt", from Marx Bros. film "The Cocoanuts", was taken from melody of Bizet's "Toreador Song" from opera "Carmen". This film reprised several Berlin numbers from the stage version.

FROM "THE MUSICAL FILM" BY DOUGLAS McVAY: "In Britain, the young Paul Robeson, in J. Elder Will's "The Song Of Freedom", does justice to Irving Berlin's "Lonely Road"...". (This was in 1936.)

The only new song written and copyrighted by Irving Berlin during 1967 was "You've Got To Be Way Out To Be In."

On TV's "The Ed Sullivan Show", May 5, 1968, six days before Berlin's 80th birthday, Robert

Goulet publicly introduced Berlin's "I Used To Be Color Blind" for the first time.